WORLD OF
KNITTED
TOYS

WORLD OF
KNITTED
TOYS

KATH DALMENY

David & Charles

For my mother, who first taught me how to wield a needle.

A DAVID & CHARLES BOOK

First published in the UK in 1998
Reprinted 1999
First paperback edition 2001
Reprinted 2003, 2006(twice)

Distributed in North America
by F&W Publications, Inc.
4700 East Galbraith Road
Cincinnati, OH 45236
1-800-289-0963

A catalogue record for this book is available from
the British Library.

ISBN 0 7153 1224 3

Photography by Alan Duns
Styling by Kath Dalmeny
Artworks by Penny Brown
Book design by StoreyBooks
Printed in Singapore by KHL printing Co Pte Ltd
for David & Charles
Brunel House   Newton Abbot   Devon

David & Charles books are available from all good book-
shops; alternatively you can contact our Orderline on
(0)1626 334555 or write to us at FREEPOST EX2 110, David
& Charles Direct, Newton Abbot, TQ12 4ZZ (no stamp
required UK mainland).

Visit our website at www.davidandcharles.co.uk

CONTENTS

INTRODUCTION

Knitted toys are always a success with children – something to love and cuddle as well as play with. And they're fun and relatively quick for you to make. In this book you'll find an exciting collection of animals from all around the world: popular choices such as kittens, baby monkeys and tiger cubs, as well as unusual ones you probably won't find anywhere else such as warthogs, chipmunks and a duck-billed platypus.

Each chapter covers a different habitat, the animals that make their homes there, and one of the people who live there, too. Each human figure is dressed in the local costume, sometimes carrying the things they use every day. The details (the Australian Sheep Farmer even has corks hanging around his hat!) and accessories will give children hours of fun.

CHOOSING A PROJECT

All the projects in the book are listed under Easy, Straightforward and Challenging to help you find the project that is right for you.

Easy!
Simple enough for the beginner to tackle.

Spider Monkey (p18)
Baby Spider Monkey (p18)
Snake (p21)
Merino Sheep (p34)
Duck-Billed Platypus (p39)
Wombat (p41)
Baby Joey (p44)
Highland Bull (p50)
Large White Pig (p52)
Tamworth Pig (p52)
Saddleback Pig (p52)
Large White Piglet (p53)
Tamworth Piglet (p53)
Saddleback Piglet (p53)
Chick (p61)
Dolphin (p65)
Shark (p67)
Octopus (p73)
Husky Dog (p113)
Fish (p114)
Adélie Penguin Chick (p118)
Seal (p119)
Sea Lion (p124)

Straightforward
Fairly easy, with one or two more challenging aspects.

South American Indian (p16)
Gorilla (p25)
Orang Utan (p26)
Parrot (p28)
Australian Sheep Farmer (p32)
Kangaroo (p43)
Farmer (p48)
Mallard Duck (p58)
Chicken (p60)
Cockerel (p61)
Pearl Fisherman (p64)
Turtle (p70)
Clownfish (p75)
Canadian Mountie (p78)
Baby Grizzly Bear (p82)
Beaver (p84)
Park Ranger (p94)
Lioness (p100)
Lion Cub (p100)
Emperor Penguin (p115)
Adélie Penguin (p115)
Emperor Penguin Chick (p116)
Walrus (p120)
Polar Bear (p122)
Panda (p125)

Challenging
Suited to the more experienced knitter.

Tiger Cub (p23)
Koala (p36)
Baby Koala (p37)
Gloucester Old Spot Pig (p55)
Gloucester Old Spot Piglet (p55)
Cat (p56)
Killer Whale (p69)
Grizzly Bear (p81)
Raccoon (p86)
Chipmunk (p88)
Moose (p90)
Zebra (p96)
Lion (p99)
Rhinoceros (p101)
Elephant (p104)
Warthog (p106)
Eskimo (p110)

MATERIALS AND EQUIPMENT

Each project lists exactly what materials and equipment you need to knit the toy and also what you will require to make most of the props pictured with the animals and people.

Yarn

Most of the projects are worked in double knitting yarn. It doesn't matter which brand you buy – choose according to the colour and texture you want. All the yarn amounts given are approximate.

Do follow yarn care instructions on the label. Most knitted toys will survive being washed in a washing machine, so long as they are not filled with kapok, and you don't spin them or spin dry them.

Needles and pins

Each pattern tells you which needles to use. It's not vital that you use the suggested needles, but remember, if you use larger needles you will need more yarn and get a bigger toy.

Always use large glass-headed or plastic-headed pins, as normal pins could get lost in the toy.

Eyes

Most toys in this book are fitted with toy safety eyes. These come as a plastic dome attached to a protruding shank. A washer is pushed over the end of the shank once the eye is in position. If you prefer, especially if you are making toys for tiny babies, you could sew simple eyes in dark or coloured yarn.

Alternatively, make felt eyes. Below are patterns for each eye size used in this book. The larger circle of each pair is for coloured felt. The smaller circle

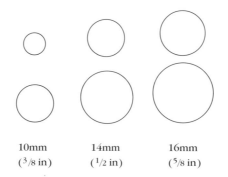

| 10mm | 14mm | 16mm |
| ($3/8$ in) | ($1/2$ in) | ($5/8$ in) |

Template for alternative felt eyes

in each pair is for a black felt pupil. Trace eye pattern pieces on to paper and cut them out. Draw round circles on felt and cut them out. Sew pupil on top of coloured circle and sew eye to face.

Stuffing

Polyester stuffing is the most suitable for knitted toys. It is safe, hygienic, washable and easy to use. Kapok tends to cover everything with fluff, come out through holes in knitting and settle into lumps inside the toy.

When stuffing small toys or awkward shapes fill area with stuffing as you sew toy up rather than attempting it at the end.

Safety guidelines

If you're making a toy for a small child, make sure all separate pieces are sewn securely in place, and leave out any additional decoration, such as beads or pipe-cleaners.

BASIC TECHNIQUES

All the techniques you need to work the projects are covered in this section: from casting on and off and basic knitting stitches, to embroidery and making up the toys. It is useful reference for experienced knitters and an essential starting point for beginners.

Knitting

The techniques used in the projects have been kept as simple as possible. Most of the toys are knitted in stocking stitch; only occasionally other stitches are introduced to add texture.

Casting on
Make a slip loop in the yarn and place the loop on the left-hand (LH) needle. Insert the right-

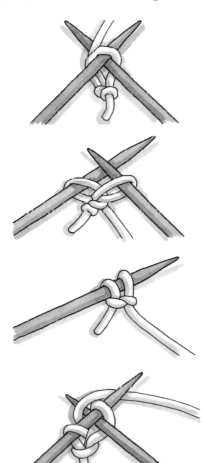

hand (RH) needle into the loop and wind the yarn around the RH needle. Pull the yarn through and put this new loop on to the LH needle. Insert the RH needle between the two stitches on the LH needle. Wind the yarn around the point of the RH needle, pull a loop through and put this on the LH needle. Repeat until you have enough stitches on the LH needle.

Casting off
Knit the first two stitches. *Using the LH needle, lift the first stitch over the second and drop it off the needle. Knit the next stitch and repeat from * until one stitch remains on the RH needle. Cut the yarn, thread it through the remaining stitch and tighten up gently.

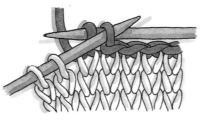

Knit stitches
Hold the needle with the cast-on stitches in your left hand. Push the RH needle through the front of the first stitch, from front to back. Wind yarn over the point

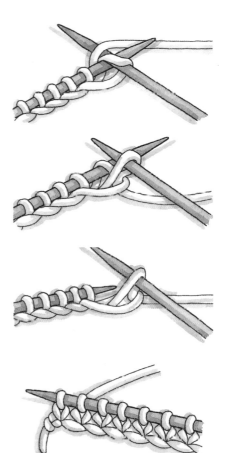

of the RH needle. Pull the RH needle with the new stitch back to the front of the work. Slip the original stitch off the LH needle, and keep the new stitch on the RH needle.

Purl stitches
Take the yarn to the front of the work. Insert the RH needle from right to left through the front of the first stitch on the LH needle. Wind the yarn from right to left over the RH needle. Pull the RH needle with the new stitch back

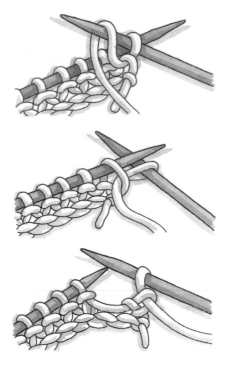

through the stitch on the LH needle. Slip the original stitch off the LH needle, and keep the new stitch on the RH needle.

Stocking stitch (st-st) – Stocking stitch combines rows of plain and purl to give one smooth side and one textured side to your work.

*Knit one row. Purl one row. Rep from * to end of work. When smooth side of work is facing you, knit that row. When textured side is facing you, purl that row.

Rib – Rib alternates knit and purl in each row. The stitches that are knitted on one row are purled on the next, and those purled on one row are knitted on the next.

On an even number of stitches, first rib row: *k1, bring yarn to front of work, p1, take yarn to back of work, rep from * to end of row; second rib row: #k1, bring yarn to front of work, p1, take yarn to back of work, rep from # to end of row. On an uneven number of stitches, second rib row would read: #p1, k1, rep from # to end of row. When there is a column of

smooth v-shaped stitches under the next stitch to be worked, knit that stitch. When there is a column of textured stitches under next stitch to be worked, purl that stitch.

Moss stitch – Moss stitch alternates knit and purl in each row, but instead of creating ribbed columns, moss stitch gives you a knobbly textured pattern.

On an even number of stitches, first moss stitch row: *k1, bring yarn to front of work, p1, take yarn to back of work, rep from * to end of row; second moss stitch row: #p1, k1, rep from # to end of row.

On an uneven number of stitches, second moss stitch row would read: #k1, p1, rep from # to end of row. When there is a smooth v-shaped stitch under next stitch to be worked, purl that stitch. When there is a textured stitch under next stitch to be worked, knit that stitch.

Joining a new colour – These toys have been designed so colour changes are only at the beginning of a new row. Work to end of row in original colour. Break off yarn, leaving a 12.5cm (5in) end. Use this later for joining. Tie new colour to original colour, with knot as close to knitting as possible. Continue work in new colour.

Markers – You'll sometimes need to recognise a particular row in your work. Using short lengths of contrasting yarn as markers, thread one through each of the two end stitches of the row indicated.

Decrease (k or p2 tog) – To knit two stitches together (k2 tog) or purl two stitches together (p2 tog), work as if two stitches are one. Push right-hand (RH) needle into stitches in the normal way, picking up both loops. Pull new stitch through both loops at once.

Increase (inc one st into next st) – On a knit row, to increase, knit into back of stitch on left-hand (LH) needle. Pull stitch on RH needle through, but do not slip stitch off LH needle in the normal way. Bring point of RH needle round and knit into front of stitch on LH needle.

To increase on a purl row, purl into back of stitch on LH needle. Pull stitch on RH needle through, but do not slip stitch off LH needle in normal way. Bring point of the RH needle round and purl into front of stitch on LH needle.

Tension (gauge) – Tension (gauge) isn't as critical for toys as for knitted garments. The tension measurements are given as a guide only. Knit more loosely for a bigger toy. Knit more tightly for a smaller toy. Yarn amounts will vary.

An approximate size for the finished projects is always given, but again this should only be used as a guide.

Embroidery

Details on the toys – such as mouths, spots and buttonholes – are all embroidered on to the knitting using simple stitches in yarn.

Chainstitch – Bring yarn up where line of chainstitch will start. *Push needle back down through place where yarn comes through knitting, and bring point of needle up 1cm (1/2in) away. Loop yarn round point of needle, then pull needle through to give a loop held in shape by yarn. Rep from * to end of chainstitch line.

Buttonhole stitch – Secure yarn near buttonhole on back of work. Bring yarn up through knitting 1cm (1/2in) from edge of hole. *Push needle down through knitting next to where yarn comes out, and bring point of needle up through hole. Loop yarn round point of needle, then pull needle through. Rep from * around hole, then secure yarn.

Lazy daisy – A lazy daisy is five chain stitches, radiating from a central point.

Swiss darning – Swiss darning mimics the texture of knitting to make markings that are hard to include in the main instructions. Each knitted stitch looks like a V. Bring yarn up through bottom point of V. Sew a stitch over left prong of V, then rep for right prong of V. On Swiss darning charts, each V stitch is represented by a square with a black blob in the middle.

Running stitch – Running stitch is a line of stitching going up and down through the knitted fabric.

Decorative touches

Single chain – Make a loop of yarn. *Pass end of yarn under hole in loop. Reach through loop and pull some yarn through, creating a new loop. Rep from * until you have the desired length. Finish by tying a knot.

Plait – A plait turns three lengths or bunches of yarn into a single decorative cord. With three lengths of yarn lying parallel, tied together at one end, *bring strand on left into middle, crossing strand next to it; then bring strand on right into middle crossing strand next to it; rep from * until you have the desired length. Tie end of plait in knot.

Pom-pom – To make a pom-pom, wrap yarn loosely round and round your fingers. Tie tightly in the centre with a separate length of yarn. Slip yarn off fingers and cut all loops. Trim pom-pom to neaten.

Making up the toys

Most of the toys are made in separate pieces which are stuffed and then joined together. Sew up using a blunt-ended needle, such as a tapestry needle, and match the colour of the yarn to your knitting.

Ladderstitch – Ladderstitch is used to join two stuffed pieces together. Hold piece 1 in position against piece 2. *Make a stitch into piece 1, move along seam (running all the way round area where two pieces touch) and make a stitch into piece 2. Rep from * until pieces are securely attached. Sew a few stitches to secure yarn.

Joining stitch – Joining stitch makes neat seams between the edges of two knitted pieces. *Thread yarn through a loop on edge of piece 1. Move along seam and thread yarn through a loop on piece 2. Rep from * to end of seam.

Bend (to form head or paw) – Head, tail or paw sections are often formed by bending a part of the work and using ladderstitch to hold it in position (see diagram below). Try to work neat, even stitches.

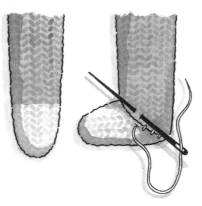

Mouth – Most mouths in this book are made with long stitches in yarn. Make stitches in thread to hold mouth in smooth curve (see diagram top right).

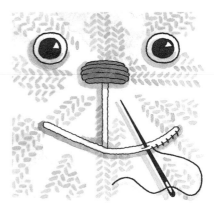

Securing yarn – After sewing with yarn, the final thing to do is take yarn through toy to a place where stitches won't show (e.g. under arm, or behind ear). Make tiny stitches on top of each other to secure yarn, then trim end.

PLEASE NOTE
If a set of instructions is given in brackets it will be followed by words telling you how many times to repeat those bracketed instructions. For instance, '(k2 tog, k2) three times' would be written in long-hand as 'k2 tog, k2, k2 tog, k2, k2 tog, k2'.

Abbreviations

alt	=	alternate
approx	=	approximately
beg	=	begin or beginning
cm	=	centimetre(s)
cont	=	continue or continuing
dec	=	decrease or decreasing
DK	=	double knit
foll	=	follow or following
g	=	gram(s)
inc	=	increase or increasing
k	=	knit
mm	=	millimetre(s)
p	=	purl
rem	=	remain or remaining
rep	=	repeat
st-st	=	stocking stitch
st	=	stitch
sts	=	stitches
tog	=	together

BASIC PERSON PATTERN

Approximate size: 29cm (11½in)

All the knitted people in the book are based on the pattern below which is for the basic person with no colour changes or clothing. Instructions for these are included in the projects for each separate person, along with a list of tools and materials suited to that toy.

Tension

Over st-st, using 3¼mm (size 10, US 3) needles, 26sts and 34 rows to 10cm (4in).

Also . . .

Figures in [square brackets] give the total number of stitches or rows you should have at that stage.

All the information you need to work the basic person is in Basic Techniques, p9–13.

BODY AND HEAD
Make one

Cast on 44sts. Working in st-st throughout and beg with a k row, work 28 rows.

Shape shoulders: Next row: k(9), k2 tog, k2 tog, k((18)), k2 tog, k2 tog, k to end of row. **Next row:** p. Rep last 2 rows, with number of sts in single brackets 1 less each time, and number of sts in double brackets 2 less each time, until 24sts rem. **Next row:** p. Mark both ends of this row with coloured yarn.

Shape chin: Next row: k1, (inc one st into next st, k2) seven times, inc one st into next st, k1; [32sts].

Next k row: k5, (inc one st into next st, k3) twice, inc one st into next st, k4, (inc one st into next st, k3) twice, inc one st into next st, k5; [38sts].

Next k row: k5, (inc one st into next st, k4) twice, inc one st into next st, k6, (inc one st into next st, k4) twice, inc one st into next st, k5; [44sts]. Work 5 rows; [10 rows total since coloured marker].

Next row: k22, turn and cast on 5sts (bottom of nose), turn and k to end of row; [49sts]. Work 3 rows; [14 rows total since coloured marker].

Shape top of nose: Next row: k22, k2 tog, k1, k2 tog, k22; [47sts].

Next k row: k21, k2 tog, k1, k2 tog, k21; [45sts]. Work 5 rows; [22 rows total since coloured marker].

Shape top of head: Next row: k5, (k2 tog, k3) seven times, k5; [38sts]. **Next k row:** k3, (k2 tog, k2) eight times, k3; [30sts]. **Next k row:** k2, (k2 tog, k1) four times, k2, (k2 tog, k1) four times, k2; [22sts].

Next k row: k3, k2 tog eight times, k3; [14sts].

Break off yarn, slip end through rem sts and pull tight. This is top of head.

With smooth sides together, fold body and head piece in half (inside out) and sew open

edge of nose closed. Turn smooth sides out and fold body and head piece in half. Starting at top of head, join long seam to run down centre of person's back. Position and fit toy safety eyes on either side of nose. Fill with stuffing then sew closed. Remove markers.

LEGS
Make two

Cast on 16sts. This is the foot end. P 1 row. Working in st-st throughout, next row: inc one st into first st, k6, inc one st into next 2sts, k6, inc one st into last st; [20sts]. Work 36 rows; [38 rows total]. Cast off.

With smooth sides outwards, fold leg piece in half. Join foot end and side seams, fill with stuffing then sew closed. Ladderstitch to body. Approx 4cm (1½ in) up from end of leg, bend foot up at right angle and ladderstitch into position.

ARMS
Make two

Cast on 14sts. P 1 row. Working in st-st throughout, next row: inc one st into first st, k5, inc one st into next 2sts, k5, inc

one st into last st; [18sts]. Work 25 rows; [27 rows total]. K2 tog at both ends and once near middle of next and every foll k row until 3sts rem. Cast off. This is the shoulder end.

With smooth sides outwards, fold arm piece in half. Join hand end and side seams, fill with stuffing then ladderstitch open end to body. About 2.5cm (1in) up from end of arm, wind matching yarn tightly round arm to form wrist. Secure end of yarn by making a few stitches.

EARS
Make two

Cast on 8sts. P 1 row. **Next row:** inc one st into first st, k6, inc one st into last st. Work 4 rows in st-st. Cast off.

With matching yarn, sew around edge of ear to neaten, then sew to side of head.

MOUTH

Make one big horizontal stitch as mouth, then secure yarn in a smooth curve with tiny stitches worked in thread (see p11).

HAIR

Make an approx 300cm (120in) single chain. With thread,

attach end of chain to head behind one ear. Sew chain to top of head in a line defining edge of hair (see diagram above).

Working inwards from this line, continue to sew chain to head, coiling it round to fill hair area. Sew final end of chain securely in position in centre of head.

For plaits (make two the same): Cut six 20cm (8in) lengths of yarn. Holding lengths in one bunch, tie in middle with another length of yarn (use this later to sew plait to head). Fold yarn in half around tie and divide 12 ends into 3 groups of 4. Plait groups together until 5cm (2in) from end (see Basic Techniques, p11). Tie end of plait in knot. Wrap coloured yarn around knot as hair tie. Sew end of plait behind ear.

IN THE JUNGLE

SOUTH AMERICAN INDIAN

Approximate size: 29cm (11½ in)

In the jungles of South America many tribes of native people still live the traditional life of the hunter-gatherer. It is a simple life in harmony with the environment – the people have respect for their surroundings and honour the lush tropical forest that provides everything they need.

This South American Indian toy is wearing a traditional costume which might be worn for a ceremony in celebration of the wonders of the South American jungle. On his shield are representations of snakes and a lizard, and in his hair are feathery emblems of the bright parrots that share his world.

How easy is it to make?

Straightforward. The pieces aren't complicated. The props and costume may take a little extra time to complete, but you could always simplify the job by leaving out some of the detailed decoration. If you're making this toy for a small child, you may want to sew the costume in place on the Indian's body, to avoid pieces getting lost.

Needles: 3 ¼mm (size 10, US 3)

Yarn: 50g DK in skin colour; 20g DK in cream (for ceremonial skirt); a small amount (less than 20g) DK in black; scraps of DK in dark brown; scraps of DK in assorted colours for designs on ceremonial skirt and shield

Pair 10mm (³/8in) toy safety eyes

Tapestry and sewing needles

Dark brown thread

Washable polyester toy stuffing

Props: cardboard for shield and spear tip; glue; double-sided tape; grey metallic paint; kebab stick for spear; small feathers or oddments of yarn

Tension

Over st-st, using 3 ¼mm (size 10, US 3) needles, 26sts and 34 rows to 10cm (4in).

Also . . .

Figures in [square brackets] give total number of stitches or rows you should have at that stage.

The Basic Person Pattern is on p12.

All the information you need to work the South American Indian is in Basic Techniques, p9–13.

BODY AND HEAD
Make one, using skin colour
Work and make up as for Basic Person pattern.

LEGS, ARMS AND EARS
Make two of each, using skin colour
Work and make up as for Basic Person Pattern, and ladderstitch to body.

CEREMONIAL SKIRT
Make two pieces, using cream
Cast on 20sts. Beg with a k row, work 22 rows. Cast off. This is the top edge.

Make a 40cm (16in) length of single chain in dark brown yarn. Lay skirt pieces next to each other, smooth sides facing up, with a 1cm (½in) gap between them. Lay chain along top edge of skirt pieces, with an even amount spare at each end. Sew chain to skirt pieces.

Embroider designs on front skirt piece in coloured yarn and Swiss darning, following chart below (see Basic Techniques, p11, and picture on p17 as guides).

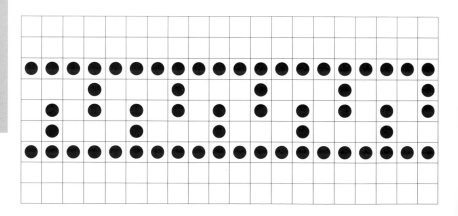

Ceremonial skirt Swiss darning chart

Ceremonial shield template (actual size)

FINISHING TOUCHES

Ceremonial shield: Trace shield design on to paper. Stick paper on to cardboard and cut it out. Stick double-sided tape all over paper and peel off backing to reveal design. Stick coloured yarn around outlines of shapes, then fill spaces with coils of yarn. Stick a loop of card to back of shield as handle.

Spear: To the top of a kebab stick, attach a small triangle of cardboard. Paint cardboard silver.

Hairband: Make a 22.5cm (9in) single chain in coloured yarn. Sew it around Indian's head. Poke small feathers into hairband or embroider long stitches radiating from hairband, in clumps, to mimic feathers.

MOUTH

Work as for Basic Person Pattern, using dark brown.

HAIR

Work as for Basic Person Pattern, using black.

SPIDER MONKEY

Approximate sizes: Mother 66.5cm (26in); Baby 43cm (17in)

The gymnasts of the jungle, spider monkeys can move with incredible speed through high branches of trees in search of the delicious tropical fruit that is their favourite food. They also enjoy playing together in the treetops, testing out their gymnastic skills by leaping through the foliage, using their powerful tails as a fifth limb and screeching with delight at the thrill of the chase.

These knitted spider monkeys have floppy limbs so they can drape themselves over a table, bed or shoulder in just the right way, or perform their own gymnastics – with a little help! They're just as happy being carried by one foot, upside down, as they are cradled in the crook of a small arm.

How easy is it to make?

Easy! The limbs, body and head, ears and tail are all rectangles with minimum shaping. Only the face has slightly more complex shaping, and the separate fingers could take a little while to make. If you find fluffy yarn hard to manage, or if you're knitting this toy for a baby, substitute brown DK yarn for mohair.

For both monkeys

Needles: 3 ¼mm (size 10, US 3)

Tapestry and sewing needles

Black thread

Washable polyester toy stuffing

For mother monkey

Yarn: 120g DK in dark brown mohair; 40g DK in mid brown; scraps of DK in black

Pair 14mm (½in) toy safety eyes

For baby monkey

Yarn: 60g DK in dark brown mohair; 20g DK in mid brown; scraps of DK in black

Pair 10mm (⅜in) toy safety eyes

Tension

Over st-st, using 3 ¼mm (size 10, US 3) needles, 26sts and 34 rows to 10cm (4in).

Also . . .

Figures in [square brackets] give total number of stitches or rows you should have at that stage.

All the information you need to work the Spider Monkeys is in Basic Techniques, page p9–13.

Making the monkeys

To make a mother monkey use the following instructions and ignore numbers in {curly brackets}. To make a baby follow the same instructions, but use the numbers in {curly brackets}.

BODY AND HEAD
Make one, using dark brown mohair

Cast on 60{40}sts. Working in st-st throughout and beg with a k row, work 100{70} rows.
Next row: (k2 tog, k26{16}, k2 tog) twice. **Next k row:** (k2 tog, k24{14}, k2 tog) twice. **Next k row:** (k2 tog, k22{12}, k2 tog) twice. **Next k row:** (k2 tog, k20{10}, k2 tog) twice. **Next k row:** (k2 tog, k18{8}, k2 tog) twice.
Next row: p. {For baby monkey: Cast off.}

For mother monkey, cont as follows. **Next row:** (k2 tog, k16, k2 tog) twice. **Next k row:** (k2 tog, k14, k2 tog) twice; [32sts]. **Next row:** p. Cast off. This is the head end.

With smooth sides together, fold body and head piece in half. Join head end and long side seam, fill with stuffing then sew bottom edge closed.

Neck: For mother monkey, approx 15cm (6in) down from top of head, sew a line of running stitch in matching yarn around body, and pull in to form neck (see Basic Techniques, p11). Secure end of yarn by making a few stitches. For baby monkey, do the same, approx 10cm (4in) down from top of head.

ARMS AND LEGS
Make four, using dark brown mohair

Cast on 30{20}sts. Beg with a k row, st-st 80{60} rows. Cast off.

With smooth sides together, fold limb piece in half. Join end and side seam, fill with stuffing then sew closed. Ladderstitch to body.

Knees and elbows: Bend arm in half and ladderstitch at crook of elbow to hold in position (see Basic Techniques, p11). Rep on backs of legs for knees.

TAIL
Make one, using dark brown mohair

Cast on 24{16}sts. Working in st-st throughout and beg with a k row, work 100{70} rows.

Next row: (k2 tog, k8{4}, k2 tog) twice. **Next k row:** (k2 tog, k6{2}, k2 tog) twice. **Next row:** p. {For baby spider monkey: Cast off.}

For mother spider monkey, cont as follows. **Next row:** (k2 tog, k4, k2 tog) twice; [12sts]. **Next row:** p. Cast off.

With smooth sides together, fold tail piece in half. Join around edge. Ladderstitch short straight edge of tail to back of body.

EARS
Make two, using mid brown

Cast on 24{16}sts. Working in st-st throughout and beg with a k {p} row, work 4{3} rows.

Next row: (k2 tog, k8{4}, k2 tog) twice. **Next row:** p. Cast off.

With smooth sides outwards, fold ear piece in half. Join around edge, then ladderstitch to side of head.

PAWS
Make four, using mid brown

Cast on 30{20}sts. Working in st-st throughout and beg with a k row, work 16{10} rows.

Next row: (k2 tog, k11{6}, k2 tog) twice. **Next k row:** (k2 tog, k9{4}, k2 tog) twice. **Next row:** p. {For baby monkey: Cast off.}

For mother monkey, cont as follows. **Next row:** (k2 tog, k7, k2 tog) twice; [18sts]. **Next row:** p. Cast off.

With smooth sides outwards, fold paw piece in half. Join around curved end and side seam, fill with stuffing then sew closed. Ladderstitch to end of limb.

FINGERS
Make twenty, using mid brown

Cast on 10{8}sts. Beg with a k row, st-st 14{10} rows. Next row: k2 tog five {four} times.

Next row: p. Break off yarn, slip end through rem sts and pull tight.

With smooth sides outwards, fold finger piece in half. Join side seam, fill with stuffing then sew closed. Ladderstitch four fingers to end of each paw. Ladderstitch one finger to base of each paw, making extra stitches to hold finger flat against palm.

FACE FOR MOTHER SPIDER MONKEY
Make one, using mid brown

Cast on 14sts. Working in st-st throughout and beg with a k row, work 2 rows.

Next row: inc one st into first 2sts, (k2, inc one st into next 2sts) three times; [22sts]. **Next k row:** inc one st into first 2sts, (k4, inc one st into next 3sts) twice, k4, inc one st into last 2sts; [32sts]. **Next k row:** k10, inc one st into next 3sts, k6, inc one st into next 3sts, k10; [38sts]. **Next k row:** k12, inc one st into next 3sts, k8, inc one st into next 3sts, k12; [44sts]. Work 7 rows; [16 rows total].

Next row: k12, k2 tog three times, k8, k2 tog three times, k12; [38sts]. **Next k row:** k10, k2 tog three times, k6, k2 tog three times, k10; [32sts]. **Next k row:** k8, k2 tog three times, k4, k2 tog three times, k8; [26sts]. Work 9 rows; [30 rows total].

Next row: k2 tog, k5, k2 tog, k8, k2 tog, k5, k2 tog; [22sts]. **Next k row:** k2 tog, k2 tog, k1, k2 tog, k8, k2 tog, k1, k2 tog, k2 tog; [16sts]. **Next row:** p. Cast off.

FACE FOR BABY SPIDER MONKEY
Make one, using mid brown

Cast on 10sts. Working in st-st throughout and beg with a k row, work 2 rows.

Next row: inc one st into first st, (k2, inc one st into next st) three times; [14sts]. **Next k row:** inc one st into first st, k2, inc one st into next 2sts, k4, inc one st into next 2sts, k2, inc one st into last st; [20sts]. **Next k row:** inc one st into first st, k4, inc one st into next 2sts, k6, inc one st into next 2sts, k4, inc one st into last st; [26sts]. Work 5 rows; [12 rows total].

Next row: k6, k2 tog, k2 tog, k6, k2 tog, k2 tog, k6; [22sts]. **Next k row:** k5, k2 tog, k2 tog, k4, k2 tog, k2 tog, k5; [18sts]. Work 7 rows; [22 rows total].

Next row: k2 tog, k3, k2 tog, k4, k2 tog, k3, k2 tog; [14sts]. **Next k row:** k2 tog three times, k2, k2 tog three times; [8sts]. **Next row:** p. Cast off.

Finishing mother and baby spider monkeys

FACE
Position and fit toy safety eyes in face piece. Pin face to front of head with smooth side outwards, leaving muzzle puffy to allow for stuffing. Ladderstitch in place, leaving an opening (see below). Remove pins. Fill face with stuffing, then sew opening closed.

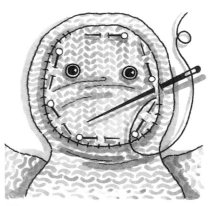

NOSTRILS AND MOUTH
With black yarn, make two or three stitches on either side of snout for nostrils. Use long straight stitches to make a mouth. Secure yarn in a smooth curve with tiny stitches worked in black thread (see Basic Techniques, p11, and picture on p19 as guides).

SNAKE

Approximate size: 90cm (35in) excluding tongue

People have always treated snakes, especially ones equipped with venomous fangs or those capable of squeezing their prey to death, with a healthy respect. Unless you know their behaviour and recognise their moods, you probably won't feel comfortable in the company of a snake. In the jungle, snakes advertise their dangerous talents by displaying fabulous colours and patterns on their skins, warning enemies not to try anything. They move slowly through the trees, winding themselves round the branches and tasting the air with their sensitive tongues to search out the small rodents and frogs that are their food.

It's a good job this knitted snake isn't poisonous and can't squeeze with its soft woolly sides. This means that it's perfectly safe to wind it round your neck or to take it to bed with you . . . At least, we hope so!

How easy is it to make?

Easy! The only shaping is at the end of the tail and for the head. Take a look at how to join new colours in Basic Techniques, p10. If you don't feel confident to do this, simply knit the whole snake in a single colour and perhaps embroider decorative patterns in chainstitch when you've finished.

Needles: 3 1/4mm (size 10, US 3)

Yarn: 20g DK in dark pink; 20g DK in white; 40g DK in black

Scraps of green and black felt

Tapestry and sewing needles

Black thread

Washable polyester toy stuffing

Tension

Over st-st, using 3 1/4mm (size 10, US 3) needles, 26sts and 34 rows to 10cm (4in).

Also . . .

Figures in [square brackets] give total number of stitches or rows you should have at that stage.

All the information you need to work the Snake is in Basic Techniques, p9–13.

BODY AND HEAD
Make one, in black, dark pink and white
Cast on 3sts in black. Working in st-st throughout and beg with a k row, work 2 rows.
Next row: inc one st into each st; [6sts]. Work 3 rows; [6 rows total]. **Next row:** inc one st into first st, k(1), inc one st into next 2sts, k to last st, inc one st into last st. Work 3 rows. Rep last 4 rows, with number of sts in brackets 2 more each time, until you have 26sts total. Work 5 rows; [28 rows total].
Working the coloured stripes: **Note** – Every time you change colour leave long ends of yarn that can be used later to sew up the snake.
The striped pattern is worked as follows: (4 rows in white; followed by 8 rows in dark pink; followed by 4 rows in white; followed by 6 rows in black). Work striped pattern in brackets ten times; [220 rows of pattern; or 248 rows total from point of tail].

Head: Cont in black, next row: inc one st into first 2sts, k9, inc one st into next 4sts, k9, inc one st into last 2sts; [34sts]. **Next k row:** inc one st into first 2sts, k13, inc one st into next 4sts, k13, inc one st into last 2sts; [42sts]. **Next k row:** inc one st into first 2sts, k17, inc one st into next 4sts, k17, inc one st into last 2sts; [50sts]. **Next k row:** inc one st into first st, k23, inc one st into next 2sts, k23, inc one st into last st; [54sts]. Work 7 rows; [20 rows total in black since final white stripe; or 262 rows in total from point of tail].
Next row: (k2 tog, k2 tog, k19, k2 tog, k2 tog) twice; [46sts]. **Next k row:** (k2 tog, k2 tog, k15, k2 tog, k2 tog) twice; [38sts]. **Next k row:** (k2 tog, k2 tog, k11, k2 tog, k2 tog) twice; [30sts]. **Next k row:** (k2 tog, k2 tog, k7, k2 tog, k2 tog) twice; [22sts]. Work 5 rows; [32 rows total in black since final white stripe; or 274 rows total from point of tail].
Next row: (k2 tog, k2 tog, k3, k2 tog, k2 tog) twice; [14sts]. **Next k row:** (k2 tog, k3, k2 tog) twice; [10sts]. **Next row:** p. Cast off.

Using long ends of yarn left when starting new colours in snake's pattern, join long straight side seam of snake, starting at tail end and stuffing snake as you work.

EYES

Trace eye pattern pieces below on to paper and cut them out. Draw round circle twice on green felt and cut out pieces. Draw round pupil shape twice on black felt and cut out pieces. Sew a pupil on to each circle, then sew circles to snake's head (see Basic Techniques, page 8).

Cut two in green	Cut two in black
◯	◇

Template for snake's eye

COLOUR VARIATIONS

The colours of this snake are based on the poisonous Garter Snake. Take a look in wildlife books to find other brightly coloured snakes to copy, and substitute your own pattern for the striped section of this snake. For more experienced knitters, invent your own snake patterns with cable stitch or perhaps Fair Isle designs in subtle greens and browns.

TONGUE

Make a 30cm (12in) length of single chain from dark pink yarn (see Basic Techniques, p10). Form into Y shape (see Diagram below) and stitch double layer of chain together to form a thick tongue. Sew tongue to front of snake's head.

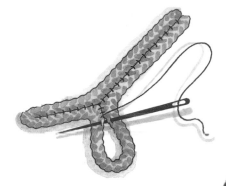

Stitch double layer of chain together to form a thick tongue

TIGER CUB

Approximate size: 20cm (8in)

Despite their terrific size (they are the largest cats on earth), tigers can pick their way silently through the jungle to creep up on their prey unawares. Their stripes of tawny orange and black help them to blend in with the shifting shadows of the undergrowth in the dense tropical jungles of India and Indonesia, earning them a place in human stories as a solitary, secretive hunter, with the power of a god.

To avoid striking fear into the nursery, this cuddly little tiger hasn't yet graduated to his full fearful powers. He's still a soft-pawed cub looking for a bit of the rough-and-tumble play that young tigers enjoy so much.

How easy is it to make?

Challenging. The legs, body and tail are straightforward, with minimal shaping. They are worked in stripes, which can become confusing for the beginner. The head and face need a little more concentration, with snout pieces that fold up and round to form the white face.

Tension

Over st-st, using 3 ¼ mm (size 10, US 3) needles, 26sts and 34 rows to 10cm (4in).

Also . . .

Figures in [square brackets] give total number of stitches or rows you should have at that stage.
   All the information you need to work the Tiger Cub is in Basic Techniques, p9–13.

Needles: *3 ¼mm (size 10, US 3)*

Yarn: *50g DK in white; 40g each DK in orange, black and yellow; scraps of DK in dark brown*

Pair 10mm (³/8in) toy safety eyes

Tapestry and sewing needles

Black thread

Washable polyester toy stuffing

TOP OF BODY AND HEAD
Make one, using yellow, orange and black
Throughout this piece, work stripes of four rows of each colour in sequence: yellow, orange and black; (see Basic Techniques, p10).

Cast on 14sts in yellow. Working in st-st and stripes throughout, and beg with a k row, work 2 rows.

Next row: k(6), inc one st into next 2sts, k to end of row. **Next row:** p. Rep last 2 rows, with number of sts in brackets 1 more each time, until you have 30sts total. Work 21 rows; [38 rows total].

Next row: k(13), k2 tog, k2 tog, k to end of row. **Next row:** p. Rep last 2 rows, with number of sts in brackets 1 less each time, until 22sts rem.

Next k row: k10, inc one st into next 2sts, k to end of row; [24sts].

Ncxt k row: k11, inc onc st into next 2sts, k to end of row. **Next k row:** k12, inc one st into next 2sts, k to end of row; [28sts]. Work 7 rows; [58 rows total].

Next row: k12, k2 tog, k2 tog, k12; [26sts]. **Next k row:** k11, k2 tog, k2 tog, k11; [24sts]. **Next k row:** k10, k2 tog, k2 tog, k10; [22sts]. **Next row:** p. Cast off. This is the head end.

BASE OF BODY AND HEAD
Make one, using white

Work as for top of head and body, but all in white, to end, but do not cast off. Mark both ends of last row with coloured yarn.

Next row: cast on 8sts, k9, k2 tog, k2 tog, k9. **Next row:** cast on 8sts, p to end of row; [36sts].

Next k row: k2 tog, (k14), k2 tog, k2 tog, k to last 2sts, k2 tog. **Next row:** p. Rep last 2 rows, with number of sts in brackets 2 less each time, until 20sts rem. Work 5 rows; [14 rows total from coloured marker].

Next row: k6, k2 tog four times, k6; [16sts]. **Next k row:** k4, k2 tog four times, k4; [12sts]. **Next row:** p. Cast off. This is the nose end.

With smooth sides outwards, join base and top pieces along one straight seam, matching head end of striped piece with coloured marker on white piece. Rep on other side of tiger.

Fold top edge of snout up to head and sew in place

Join tops of two flaps forming tiger's snout. Position and fit toy safety eyes. Fold top edge of snout up to head and sew in place (see above). Fill snout, head and body with stuffing, then sew closed. Remove coloured markers.

LEGS
Make four, using white, yellow, orange and black

Cast on 12sts in white. Working in st-st throughout and beg with a k row, work 2 rows.

Next row: inc one st into first st, k(4), inc one st into next 2sts, k to last st, inc one st into last st. **Next row:** p. Rep last 2 rows, with number of sts in brackets 2 more each time, until you have 28sts total. Work 7 rows; [16 rows total].

Change to yellow. Work stripes of four rows of each colour, in sequence: yellow, orange and black as follows. Work 22 rows. K2 tog at both ends and once near middle of next and every foll k row until 16sts rem. **Next row:** p. Cast off.

With smooth sides outwards, fold leg piece in half. With white, join end and side of paw. With orange, join side seam. Fill with stuffing then sew closed and ladderstitch to body.

Bend white paw up at right angles to leg and ladderstitch in position.

TAIL
Make one, using orange, yellow and black

Throughout this piece, work stripes of four rows of each colour in sequence: orange, yellow and black.

Cast on 14sts in orange. Working in st-st throughout and beg with a k row, work 26 rows.

Next row: k2 tog seven times; [7sts]. Break off yarn, slip end through rem sts and pull tight.

With smooth sides outwards, fold tail piece in half. With orange yarn, join long side seam. Fill with stuffing and sew open end to back of body.

EARS
Make two, using yellow, orange, and black

Cast on 20sts in yellow. Working in st-st throughout and beg with a k row, work 4 rows.

Change to orange and work 2 rows. **Next row:** (k2 tog, k6, k2 tog) twice; [16sts]. **Next row:** p. Change to black. **Next row:** (k2 tog, k4, k2 tog) twice; [12sts]. **Next row:** p. Cast off.

With smooth sides outwards, fold ear piece in half. With black yarn, join top of ear. With orange yarn, join remaining edges of ear and ladderstitch to head.

NOSE, MOUTH AND CLAWS

With brown yarn, make four or five stitches on end of snout for nose. Sew one stitch down from nose, and two big lines outwards from bottom of this stitch as a mouth. Secure yarn in a smooth curve with tiny stitches worked in black thread (see Basic Techniques, p11). On each paw, sew three straight stitches for claws (see picture on p23 as guide).

GORILLA

Approximate size: 52.5cm (21in)

Gorillas spend their lives travelling together through the jungle in close family groups, living quietly and contentedly as they forage for tasty fruit and leaves. At night they make nests to sleep in – cushions of branches and leaves piled up to keep themselves off the cold ground or to stop themselves rolling down a steep slope.

Gorillas are thoughtful and intelligent creatures – and some individuals in captivity have been taught to communicate with symbols in a very basic way, even stringing symbols into simple sentences. But the big eloquent faces of the captive gorillas, with deepset eyes and mournful expressions, often make people feel sad. They know that the gorilla should really be roaming free in the jungle that is their true home.

How easy is it to make?

Straightforward. The limbs, ears, tail, body and head are all rectangles with minimum shaping. Only the face has slightly more complex shaping, with its characteristic ridges. The paws have been kept simple with only the thumb knitted as a separate piece.

More experienced knitters might like to make paws with separate fingers, for which instructions are included.

If you find fluffy yarn hard to manage, or if you're making this toy for a baby, substitute black DK yarn for the mohair.

Needles: 3 1/4mm (size 10, US 3)

Yarn: For the gorilla: 120g DK in black mohair; 40g DK in dark grey; scraps of DK in black and mid grey. For the banana: scraps of DK in yellow, black and white

Pair 14mm (1/2in) toy safety eyes

Tapestry and sewing needles

Black thread

Washable polyester toy stuffing

Tension

Over st-st, using 3 1/4mm (size 10, US 3) needles, 26sts and 34 rows to 10cm (4in).

Also . . .

Figures in [square brackets] give the total number of stitches or rows you should have at that stage.

All the information you need to work the Gorilla is in Basic Techniques, p9–13.

BODY AND HEAD
Make one, using black mohair
Cast on 60sts. Working in st-st throughout and beg with a k row, work 100 rows.
Next row: k2 tog, k(26), k2 tog, k2 tog, k to last 2sts, k2 tog.
Next row: p. Rep last 2 rows, with number of sts in brackets 2 less each time, until 32sts rem. **Next row:** p. Cast off. This is the head end.
With smooth sides together, fold body and head piece in half. Join top of head and long side seam. Fill with stuffing then sew closed.
Neck: About 15cm (6in) down from top of head, sew a line of running stitch in matching yarn around body, and pull in to form neck (see Basic

Techniques, p11). Secure end of yarn by making a few stitches.

ARMS
Make two, using black mohair
Cast on 30sts. Beg with a k row, st-st 80 rows. Cast off.
With smooth sides together, fold arm piece in half. Join end and long side seam. Fill with stuffing then sew closed. Ladderstitch to body.
Elbows: Bend arm in half and ladderstitch at crook of elbow to hold in position (see Basic Techniques, p11).

LEGS
Make two, using black mohair
Cast on 30sts. Beg with a k row, st-st 50 rows. Cast off.
Make up as for arm and ladderstitch to body. Make knee as for elbow.

EARS
Make two, using dark grey
Cast on 24sts. Beg with a k row, st-st 4 rows.
Next row: (k2 tog, k8, k2 tog) twice; [20sts]. **Next row:** p. Cast off.
With smooth sides outwards, fold ear piece in half. Join around edge, then ladderstitch to side of head.

PAWS

Make four, using dark grey

This is a simple paw pattern that, when made up, represents the gorilla's paw and fingers. The thumb is knitted as a separate piece.

Cast on 26sts. Beg with a k row, st-st 30 rows.

Next row: (k2 tog, k9, k2 tog) twice; [22sts]. **Next row:** p. Cast off.

To make a more complex paw, with all fingers and thumb knitted as separate pieces, work as follows: Cast on 26sts. Beg with a k row, st-st 16 rows. **Next row:** (k2 tog, k9, k2 tog) twice; [22sts]. **Next row:** p. Cast off.

With smooth sides outwards, fold paw piece in half. Join end and long side seam, fill with stuffing then sew bottom edge closed. Ladderstitch bottom edge to end of limb.

FINGERS

For a simple paw: Sew a horizontal line across paw 4cm (1 ¹/₂in) from top edge. Sew three lines of stitches from curved edge of paw down to meet horizontal line, forming finger ridges.

Ladderstitch thumb to base of paw, making extra stitches to hold thumb flat against palm.

For a paw with separate fingers, follow instructions for mother spider monkey's paws and fingers, p20.

THUMBS

Make four, using dark grey

Cast on 10sts. Beg with a k row, st-st 14 rows.

Next k row: k2 tog five times. **Next row:** p. Break off yarn, slip end through rem sts and pull tight.

For a more complex paw, with all fingers and thumb knitted as separate pieces, make twenty thumb pieces in total for fingers and thumbs.

FACE

Make one, using dark grey

Work as for mother spider monkey face, p20, using dark grey yarn. Attach face as for mother spider monkey.

EYEBROWS

Make two, using dark grey

Cast on 12sts. St-st 4 rows. Cast off.

Sew eyebrow piece above eye, leaving middle slightly puffy to make it stand out.

NOSTRIL RIDGES

Make two, using dark grey

Cast on 8sts. St-st 4 rows. Cast off.

Sew nostril ridge on one side of snout, leaving middle slightly puffy to make it stand out.

NOSTRILS AND MOUTH

With black yarn, make two or three stitches under each nostril ridge. With mid grey yarn, use long straight stitches to make a mouth. Secure yarn in smooth curve with tiny stitches worked in black thread (see Basic Techniques, p11, and picture opposite as guide).

ORANG UTAN

The gorilla pattern can also be used to make an orang utan. Simply substitute black mohair with ginger, and dark grey DK yarn with mid brown. Sew nostrils and mouth in black yarn. The orang utan in the photo was made with the more complex paw pattern, with separate fingers and thumbs. The gorilla was made with the simpler paw pattern, in which fingers and paws are knitted as the same piece.

BANANA

CENTRE

Make one, using white

Cast on 6sts. Working in st-st throughout and beg with a k row, work 2 rows.

Next row: inc one st into first st, k1, inc one st into next 2sts, k1, inc one st into last st; [10sts]. Work 13 rows; [16 rows total].

Next row: (k2 tog, k1, k2 tog) twice. **Next row:** k2 tog three times. Break off yarn, slip end through rem sts and pull tight.

Fold centre piece in half and join along side seam. Fill with stuffing, then sew closed.

SKIN

Make three pieces, using yellow

Cast on 3sts. Working in st-st throughout and beg with a k row, work 2 rows. **Next row:** inc one st into first st, k1, inc one st into last st; [5sts]. Work 15 rows; [18 rows total]. **Next row:** k2 tog, k1, k2 tog. **Next row:** k3 tog. Break off yarn, slip end through rem sts and pull tight.

Join two skin pieces tog approx halfway along their length. Join third skin piece to other side of first skin piece, wrap the whole skin around the centre, then sew in place. With black yarn, embroider dark markings on the end and along sides of banana.

PARROT

Approximate size: 38cm (15in)

It's quite clear that parrots aren't afraid of anyone. In the jungle, if there are creatures watching out for a tasty supper it's best to develop camouflage if you want to stay alive. And that's just what other jungle creatures have done. There are moths that look like bark, and insects that look so like the leaves of the trees they inhabit that you'd never even notice they were there. So the brilliant plumage of the parrots is a sign that they have few natural enemies to worry about – they can afford to be noticed. This brightly coloured parrot is a Scarlet Macaw. It has been designed so that it can balance well on the edge of a bed, on the back of a chair – or even on your shoulder, if you happen to be a pirate!

How easy is it to make?

Straightforward. To make ridged feather-like wings, you'll need to be able to work in rib stitch (see Basic Techniques, p10, for step-by-step instructions).

Needles: 3 1/4mm (size 10, US 3)

Yarn: 50g DK in red; a small amount (less than 10g) DK in brown; scraps of DK in yellow, blue, black and white

Pair 10mm (3/8in) toy safety eyes

Tapestry needle

Washable polyester toy stuffing

Tension

Over st-st, using 3 1/4mm (size 10, US 3) needles, 26sts and 34 rows to 10cm (4in).

Also . . .

Figures in [square brackets] give the total number of stitches or rows you should have at that stage.

All the information you need to work the Parrot is in Basic Techniques, p9–13.

BODY AND HEAD
Make one, using red
Cast on 16sts. This is the head end. P 1 row. Working in st-st throughout, next row: inc one st into first st, k(6), inc one st into next 2sts, k to last st, inc one st into last st. Rep last 2 rows, with number of sts in brackets 2 more each time, until you have 32sts total. Work 9 rows; [17 rows total].
K2 tog at both ends of next and every foll k row until 24sts rem. Inc one st at both ends of next and every foll k row until you have 46sts total. Work 25 rows; [71 rows total].
Next row: k2 tog, k2 tog, k to last 4sts, k2 tog, k2 tog. Next row: p. Rep last 2 rows until 30sts rem.
K2 tog at both ends of next and every foll alt k row until 8sts rem. **Next row:** p. Break off yarn, slip end through rem sts and pull tight. This is the tail end.
With smooth sides outwards, fold body and head piece in half. Join long side seam, fill with stuffing then sew closed. About 7.5cm (3in) from front of head, bend head section down at right angle to body (see Basic Techniques, p11) and ladderstitch in position.

WINGS
Make two, using red, yellow and blue
The wings are knitted in a combination of smooth stocking stitch (st-st) and ridged rib stitch (rib). See Basic Techniques, p10, for step-by-step instructions for these stitches.
Left wing: cast on 12sts. Beg with a k row, st-st 2 rows. Inc one st at both ends of next and every foll k row until you have 18sts total.
Start of rib pattern (see Basic Techniques, p10). **Rib row:** *k1, p1, rep from * to end of row. Rep rib row three more times. Change to yellow and work 4 rows in rib. Change to blue and work 4 rows in rib. Change to red and work 4 rows in rib#.
Cont in rib, keeping rib pattern correct. **Next row:** k2 tog, rib to end of row. Work 3 rows; [17sts]. Rep last 4 rows.
Next row: k2 tog, rib to end of row. **Next row:** rib. Rep last 2 rows until 3sts rem. Break off yarn, slip end through rem sts and pull tight.
Right wing: work as for left wing to #. Cont in rib, keeping rib pattern correct as for left wing, above, next row: rib to last 2sts, k2 tog. Work 3

rows in rib; [17sts]. Rep last 4 rows; [16sts].

Next row: rib to last 2sts, k2 tog. **Next row:** rib. Rep last 2 rows until 3sts rem. Break off yarn, slip end through rem sts and pull tight.

Hide loose ends of yarn by sewing them back through knitting. Sew top and back of wing (down to bottom of blue stripe) to side of parrot. Tuck a little stuffing or spare red wool up under top of wing to form shoulder shape. To keep wings neatly in place, sew points of wings to back of parrot.

TOES
Make six, using brown

Cast on 8sts. Working in st-st throughout and beg with a k row, work 12 rows.

Next row: k2 tog, k to last 2sts, k2 tog. **Next row:** p. Rep last 2 rows; [4sts]. Break off yarn, slip end through rem sts and pull tight.

With smooth sides outwards, fold a toe piece in half. Join seam, fill with stuffing and sew closed.

Foot: sew three toes together with ladderstitch, working a little way up towards points of toes to make them point forwards. Ladderstitch foot in position (see picture as guide).

BEAK
Make one, using brown

Cast on 20sts. Working in st-st throughout and beg with a k row, work 8 rows.

Next row: cast on 3sts, k6, k2 tog four times, k to end of row; [19sts]. **Next row:** cast on 3sts, p to end of row; [22sts]. **Next row:** k7, k2 tog four times, k to end of row; [18sts]. **Next k row:** k5, k2 tog four times, k to end of row; [14sts]. **Next row:** p. Cast off.

With smooth sides outwards, fold beak piece in half. Join side seam, fill with stuffing then sew open end to front of head.

EYE PATCHES
Make two, using white

Cast on 4sts. P1 row. Working in st-st throughout, next row: inc one st into first st, k to last st, inc one st into last st. Rep last 2 rows; [8sts]. Work 3 rows; [7 rows total].

Next row: k2 tog, k to last 2sts, k2 tog. **Next row:** p. Rep last 2 rows; [4sts]. Cast off.

Position and fit toy safety eye in centre of eye patch. Hold eye patch in place on parrot's head, pushing shank of eye into side of head. Sew patch in position.

MOUTH AND NOSTRILS

With black yarn, make sts on either side of beak for nostrils. Sew a line of black along each side of beak (see picture as guide).

AUSTRALIAN OUTBACK

AUSTRALIAN SHEEP FARMER

Approximate size: 29cm (11½ in)

It's a lonely life being a sheep farmer in the Australian Outback. The farms are so vast that their nearest neighbours can live many miles away, and even the doctors have to make special visits by aircraft to do their rounds. So excuses for social events and communal work are always welcome. Occasions like sheep-shearing let the farmers get together to swap stories and jokes as they do the hot work of clipping the heavy fleeces from their many thousands of sheep.

This Australian sheep farmer knows how to deal with the hot weather. Wearing a short-sleeved check shirt under his jacket, and a hat to keep off the burning sun (complete with dangling corks to keep the flies out of his eyes), he's well prepared for a long Australian summer.

How easy is it to make?

Straightforward. The pieces aren't complicated. The hat and patterned shirt may take a little extra time, but you could always simplify the job by giving your farmer a plain shirt. If you're making this toy for a small child you could leave out the corks and sew the costume in place on the sheep farmer's body, to avoid pieces getting lost.

> *Needles: 3¼mm (size 10, US 3)*
>
> *Yarn: 50g DK in skin colour; 40g DK in brown; 20g each DK in dark brown, dark pink and black; a small amount (less than 20g each) DK in mid pink and brown*
>
> *Pair 10mm (³/8 in) toy safety eyes*
>
> *Tapestry and sewing needles*
>
> *Dark brown thread*
>
> *Washable polyester toy stuffing*
>
> *Three 10mm (³/8 in) diameter wooden beads*
>
> *Props: small pieces of cork for hat*

Tension

Over st-st, using 3¼mm (size 10, US 3) needles, 26sts and 34 rows to 10cm (4in).

Also . . .

Figures in [square brackets] give the total number of stitches or rows you should have at that stage.

The Basic Person Pattern is on page p12.

All the information you need to work the Sheep Farmer is in Basic Techniques, p9–13.

BODY AND HEAD
Make one, using dark brown, dark pink and skin colour
Work as for Basic Person pattern using the following colours: first 12 rows in dark brown; next section in dark pink to 'Shape chin'; rem rows in skin colour. Make up as for Basic Person pattern.

LEGS
Make two, using black and dark brown
Work as for Basic Person pattern using the following colours: first 22 rows in black; rem rows in dark brown. Make up as for Basic Person pattern and ladderstitch to body.

ARMS
Make two, using skin colour and dark pink
Cast on 14sts in skin colour. P 1 row. **Next row:** inc one st into first st, k5, inc one st into next 2sts, k5, inc one st into last st; [18sts]. Work 22 rows in st-st, ending with a k row.
Change to dark pink. K 1 row. P 1 row. K 1 row.
K2 tog at both ends and near middle of next and every foll k row until 3sts rem. Cast off.
Make up as for Basic Person pattern and ladderstitch to body.

EARS
Make two, using skin colour
Work and make up as for Basic Person pattern and sew to sides of head.

CHECKED SHIRT
Using mid pink yarn, embroider lines of chainstitch (see Basic Techniques, p10) in criss-cross pattern on dark pink areas.

JACKET SLEEVES
Make two, using brown
Cast on 26sts. K 2 rows.
Working in st-st throughout and beg with a k row, work 20 rows; [22 rows total].
K2 tog at both ends and once near middle of next and every foll k row until 11sts rem, ending with a k row. K 2 rows. Cast off.
With smooth sides out, fold sleeve piece in half and join side seam to start of shaping.

JACKET RIGHT FRONT
Make one, using brown
Cast on 14sts. K 2 rows. Working in st-st throughout and beg with a k row, work 22 rows; [24 rows total].
K2 tog at end of next and every foll k row until 8sts rem, ending with a k row. K 2 rows. Cast off.

JACKET LEFT FRONT
Make one, using brown
Cast on 14sts. K 2 rows. Working in st-st throughout and beg with a k row, work 8 rows.
The next 2 rows will make the first buttonhole, near the edge of the jacket front.
First buttonhole row: *k to last 3sts. From left, imagine rem sts are numbered 1, 2 & 3. Knit sts 3 and 2, pass st 3 over st 2 (cast it off), then k st 1.
Second buttonhole row: p2, turn and cast on one st, turn and p to end of row. Work 8 rows; [20 rows total].
To make the second buttonhole, rep first and second buttonhole rows.
Work 2 rows. K2 tog at beg of next and every foll k row until 10sts rem.
To make the third buttonhole, next k row: k2 tog, rep from * to end of first buttonhole row. Rep second buttonhole row.
Next row: k2 tog, k to end of row. K 2 rows. Cast off.
Sew around buttonholes using buttonhole stitch (see Basic Techniques, p10).

JACKET BACK
Make one, using brown
Cast on 32sts. K 2 rows. Working in st-st throughout and beg with a k row, work 22 rows.
Next row: cast off 3sts, k to end of row; [29sts]. **Next row:** cast off 3sts, p to end of row; [26sts]. K2 tog at both ends of next and every foll k row until 14sts rem. K 2 rows. Cast off.
Lay jacket back with smooth side down. With smooth sides up, lay jacket left and right front pieces on top of jacket back, with long straight edges overlapping in centre. Join side seams up to start of shaping. Position sleeves on either side of jacket and join sleeves to armholes of jacket.

HAT BRIM
Make one, using brown
Cast on 108sts. K 2 rows. Working in st-st and beg with a k row, **next row:** (k2 tog, k14, k2 tog) six times; [96sts].
Next k row: (k2 tog, k12, k2 tog) six times; [84sts]. **Next k row:** (k2 tog, k10, k2 tog) six times; [72sts]. **Next k row:** (k2 tog, k8, k2 tog) six times; [60sts]. **Next row:** p. Cast off.
Join short straight edges of brim to form full circle.

HAT TOP
Make one, using brown
Cast on 60sts. Working in st-st throughout and beg with a k row, work 4 rows.
Next row: (k2 tog, k6, k2 tog) six times; [48sts]. **Next k row:** (k2 tog, k4, k2 tog) six times; [36sts]. **Next k row:** (k2 tog, k2, k2 tog) six times; [24sts]. **Next k row:** k2 tog twelve times; [12sts]. **Next row:** p. Break off yarn, slip end through rem sts and pull tight.
With smooth sides outwards, fold hat piece in half. Join side seam to form dome. Sew base of dome to inner edge of brim.
Work a line of running stitch (see Basic Techniques, p11) close to outer edge of hat brim in brown yarn. Pull yarn gently to strengthen and straighten outer edge of brim. Secure end of yarn by making a few stitches.

MOUTH
Work as for Basic Person pattern, using dark brown.

HAIR
Work as for Basic Person pattern, using brown.

FINISHING TOUCH
Hang small pieces of cork, trimmed from wine corks, around brim of hat on short lengths of thread.

MERINO SHEEP

Approximate size: 30cm (12in)

Prized for their wool, which has very long fibres, merino sheep are farmed in vast flocks in Australia and New Zealand. Wool of such quality makes excellent fibres for warm winter clothing and thick felt to line coats and hiking boots. With his magnificent horns, this sheep is probably the leader of his flock, watching out for marauding dingo dogs that might carry off a new-born lamb. He is knitted in fuzzy textured yarn to mimic the dense fleece that makes the merino sheep so valuable to their farmers. This sheep has been designed to be large enough to cuddle, but if you'd like to make one small enough for your sheep farmer to look after, try knitting this pattern in thinner (two- or three-ply) yarn on 2 ³⁄₄mm (size 12, US 1) needles.

How easy is it to make?

Easy! The shaping is very simple and the horns, although they look difficult, are actually long, thin knitted sausage shapes coiled on the side of the sheep's head and sewn in position.

Needles: 3 ¹⁄₄mm (size 10, US 3)

Yarn: 50g DK textured yarn in cream; 20g DK yarn in cream; a small amount (less than 10g) DK yarn in pale brown; scraps of DK yarn in dark brown

Pair 14mm (¹⁄₂ in) toy safety eyes

Tapestry needle

Washable polyester toy stuffing

Tension

Over st-st, using 3 ¹⁄₄mm (size 10, US 3) needles, 26sts and 34 rows to 10cm (4in).

Also . . .

Figures in [square brackets] give the total number of stitches or rows you should have at that stage.

All the information you need to work the Merino Sheep is in Basic Techniques, p9–13.

BODY

Make one, using textured yarn

Cast on 30sts. Working in st-st throughout and beg with a k row, work 2 rows.

Next row: inc one st into first 2sts, k(11), inc one st into next 4sts, k to last 2sts, inc one st into last 2sts. **Next row:** p. Rep last 2 rows, with number of sts in brackets 4 more each time, until you have 54sts total.

Next k row: inc one st into first st, k25, inc one st into next 2sts, k to last st, inc one st into last st; [58sts]. Work 41 rows; [50 rows total].

K2 tog at both ends of next and every foll alt k row until 24sts rem. **Next k row:** (k2 tog, k8, k2 tog) twice; [20sts]. **Next row:** p. Cast off. This is the neck end.

With smooth sides together, fold body piece in half. Join neck end and side seams, fill with stuffing then sew closed.

FACE

Make one, using cream DK

Cast on 32sts. Working in st-st throughout and beg with a k row, work 2 rows.

K2 tog at both ends of next and every foll alt k row until 22sts rem. Work 3 rows. **Next row:** (k2 tog, k7, k2 tog) twice; [18sts]. **Next row:** p. Cast off. This is the nose end.

With smooth sides outwards, fold face piece in half. Join nose end and side seams. Position and fit toy safety eyes. Fill with stuffing, then sew open end to neck end of body (see picture opposite as guide).

LEGS

Make four, using cream DK and textured yarn

Cast on 16sts in cream DK yarn. Working in st-st throughout and beg with a k row, work 4 rows. Inc one st at both ends of next and every foll alt k row, until you have 24sts. Work 3 rows, ending with a p row.

Change to textured yarn and beg with a p row, st-st 10 rows. Cast off.

With smooth sides of cream DK section outwards, fold leg piece in half. Join narrow end and side seams. Fill with stuffing, then sew closed. Ladderstitch to body.

Sew a 2.5cm (1in) line of stitches up at right angles from base of foot to form hoof (see picture opposite as guide).

HORNS

Make two, using pale brown

Cast on 12sts. Working in st-st throughout and beg with a k row, work 50 rows.

*Next row: (k2 tog, k2, k2 tog) twice; [8sts]. Next k row: k2 tog four times; [4sts]. Break off yarn, slip end through rem sts and pull tight.

With smooth sides outwards, fold horn piece in half. Join long straight seam, fill with stuffing then sew closed. Ladderstitch straight end of horn to side of sheep's head. Coil horn and hold in position with stitches where the horn touches the head, and where the horn touches itself (see below).

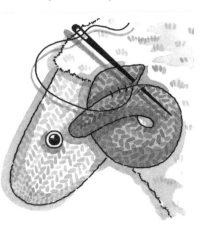

TAIL

Make one, using textured yarn

Cast on 12sts. Beg with a k row, st-st 18 rows. Work as for horns from * to end.

With smooth sides together, fold tail piece in half. Join around edge, then ladderstitch to back of sheep.

MOUTH AND NOSTRILS

With brown yarn, make two or three stitches on either side of nose as nostrils. Use long straight stitches to make a mouth (see Basic Techniques, p11, and picture below as guides).

KOALA

Approximate sizes: Mother 30cm (12in); Baby 19cm (7 1/2 in)

Like kangaroos, mother koalas carry their baby in their pouch during its early life. Soon the baby outgrows the pouch and has to cling on hard to its mother's back as she makes her way through the trees in search of juicy eucalyptus leaves. But it's a slow search, because koalas don't move fast, and often stop to nap in the fork of a branch. In fact, koalas sleep for up to eighteen hours a day! In the heat of the Australian Outback, they can often be seen snoozing in the tree's shade, which has given rise to the story (wholly unfair) that they are drugged by the eucalyptus leaves that they feed on.

How easy is it to make?

Challenging. The limbs, body, ears and nose are all simple pieces with minimum shaping. Only the face has slightly more complex shaping, and the fluffy pom-pom ears are an unusual technique.

For both koalas

Needles: 3 1/4mm (size 10, US 3)

Tapestry and sewing needles

Black thread

Washable polyester toy stuffing

For the mother koala

Yarn: 70g DK in mid grey; scraps of DK in dark brown, pale grey and black

(One 100g ball of mid grey is enough to make a mother and baby koala)

Pair 14mm (1/2 in) toy safety eyes

For the baby koala

Yarn: 40g DK in mid grey; scraps of DK in dark brown, pale grey and black

Pair 10mm (3/8 in) toy safety eyes

Tension

Over st-st, using 3 1/4mm (size 10, US 3) needles, 26sts and 34 rows to 10cm (4in).

Also . . .

Figures in [square brackets] give the total number of stitches or rows you should have at that stage.

All the information you need to work these Koalas is in Basic Techniques, p9–13.

Making the koalas

Make body and head for either mother or baby. Then make arms, legs, ears and nose, ignoring numbers in {curly brackets} for the mother, and using the numbers in {curly brackets} for the baby.

BODY AND HEAD FOR MOTHER
Make one, using mid grey
Cast on 28sts. Working in st-st throughout and beg with a k row, work 2 rows.
Next row: inc one st into first 2sts, k(10), inc one st into next 4sts, k(10), inc one st into last 2sts. **Next k row:** p. Rep last 2 rows, with number of sts in brackets 4 more each time, until you have 52sts total.
Next k row: inc one st into first st, k24, inc one st into next 2sts, k24, inc one st into last st; [56sts]. Work 25 rows; [34 rows total].
Next row: k2 tog, k(24), k2 tog, k2 tog, k to last 2sts, k2 tog. **Next row:** p. Rep last two rows, with number of sts in brackets 2 less each time, until 36sts rem. This is the neck.
Next k row: inc one st into first st, k(5), inc one st into next 2sts, k2, inc one st into next 2sts, k(5), inc one st into next 2sts, k to last stitch, inc one st into last st. **Next row:** p. Rep last 2 rows, with number of sts in brackets 3 more each time, until you have 68sts total.
Next k row: inc one st into first st, k18, inc one st into next st, k2, inc one st into next st, k18, inc one st into next 2sts, k24, inc one st into last st; [74sts]. Work 5 rows [58 rows total].
Next row: k2 tog, k18, k2 tog, k2, k2 tog, k18, k2 tog, k2 tog, k to last 2sts, k2 tog; [68sts].
Next k row: k2 tog, k(14), k2 tog, k2 tog, k2, k2 tog, k2 tog, k(14), k2 tog, k2 tog, k to last 2sts, k2 tog; [60sts]. **Next row:** p. Rep last 2 rows, with number of sts in brackets 3 less each time, until 36sts rem. **Next row:** p. Cast off. This is the top of the head.
With smooth sides outwards, fold body and head piece in half. Join base and long side seam. Fit toy safety eyes on either side of nose bulge. With nose bulge facing forwards, join top of head, fill with stuffing then sew closed.
Neck: About 12.5cm (5in) down from top of head, sew a line of running stitch in matching yarn around narrow neck

section, and pull in to form neck (see Basic Techniques, p11). Secure end of yarn by making a few stitches.

BODY AND HEAD FOR BABY
Make one, using mid grey

Cast on 18sts. Working in st-st throughout and beg with a k row, work 2 rows.

Next row: inc one st into first 2sts, k5, inc one st into next 4sts, k5, inc one st into last 2sts; [26sts]. **Next k row:** inc one st into first 2sts, k9, inc one st into next 4sts, k9, inc one st into last 2sts; [34sts]. **Next k row:** inc one st into first st, k15, inc one st into next 2sts, k to last st, inc one st into last st; [38sts]. Work 17 rows; [24 rows total].

Next row: k2 tog, k(15), k2 tog, k2 tog, k to last 2sts, k2 tog. **Next row:** p. Rep last two rows, with number of sts in brackets 2 less each time, until 22sts rem. This is the neck.

Next k row: inc one st into first st, k(2), inc one st into next 2sts, k1, inc one st into next 2sts, k(2), inc one st into next 2sts, k to last st, inc one st into last st. **Next row:** p. Rep last 2 rows, with number of sts in brackets 3 more each time, until you have 46sts total. Work 3 rows; [40 rows total].

Next row: k2 tog, k(8), k2 tog, k2 tog, k2, k2 tog, k2 tog, k(8), k2 tog, k2 tog, k to last 2sts, k2 tog. **Next row:** p. Rep last 2 rows, with number of sts in brackets 3 less each time, until 22sts rem. **Next row:** p. Cast off. This is the top of the head.

With smooth sides outwards, fold body and head piece in half. Join base and long side seam. Position and fit toy safety eyes on either side of nose bulge. With nose bulge facing forwards, join top of head, fill with stuffing then sew closed.

Neck: About 7.5cm (3in) down from top of head, sew a line of running stitch in matching yarn around narrow neck section, and pull in to form neck (see Basic Techniques, p11). Secure end of yarn by making a few stitches.

ARMS
Make two, using mid grey

Cast on 28{18}sts. Working in st-st throughout and beg with a k row, work 14{10} rows.

K2 tog at both ends of next and every foll k row until 18{12}sts rem. Work 8{6} rows. Cast off.

With smooth sides outwards, fold arm piece in half. Join narrow end and long side seam, fill with stuffing then sew closed. Ladderstitch fat end to body.

LEGS
Make two, using mid grey

Cast on 28{18}sts. Working in st-st throughout, and beg with a k row, work 24{16} rows.

K2 tog at both ends of next and every foll k row until 18{12}sts rem. Work 8{6} rows. Cast off.

Make up as for arm and ladderstitch to body.

Knees: Bend leg in half downwards at a shallow angle and ladderstitch at crook of knee to hold in position (see Basic Techniques, p11).

EARS
Make four, using mid grey

Cast on 8{5}sts. Working in st-st throughout and beg with a k row, work 6{4} rows.

K2 tog at both ends of next and every foll k row until 4{3}sts rem. **Next row:** p. Cast off.

NOSE
Make one, using dark brown

Cast on 4{3}sts. P 1 row. Working in st-st throughout, inc one st at both ends of next and every foll k row until you have 8{5}sts total. Work 7{5} rows. K2 tog at both

ends of next and every foll k row until 4{3}sts rem. **Next row:** p. Cast off.

Pin nose piece to face with smooth side outwards (see picture on p37 as guide). Sew in place and remove pins.

Finishing mother and baby koalas

EARS

For mother koala, with a mixture of mid grey and pale grey yarn, make a large shaggy pom-pom, about 10cm (4in) across (see Basic Techniques, p11). For baby koala, make a pom-pom 5cm (2in) across. Sandwich middle of pom-pom inside two ear pieces, leaving shaggy ends of yarn showing around curved edge of ear. Sew top ear piece to bottom ear piece, catching pom-pom in place (see diagram below). Ladderstitch smooth straight edge of ear to koala's head.

CLAWS AND MOUTH

On each paw, sew three straight stitches in black yarn for claws, and straight stitches at base of nose for nostrils (see picture on p37 as guide). Sew a long straight stitch for a mouth. Secure yarn in a smooth curve with tiny stitches worked in black thread (see Basic Techniques, p11).

DUCK-BILLED PLATYPUS

Approximate size: 35cm (14in) including tail

The duck-billed platypus is an extraordinary creature. When explorers from Britain first returned from Australia with a specimen to show to their scientific colleagues, they were accused of presenting a fake animal sewn together from other animal parts. The body of a mammal and the beak and feet of a duck? Preposterous! But the platypus is real and spends its life scooping up insect larvae from the bottoms of rivers and lakes, searching them out with its incredibly sensitive bill. Its dense fur, which protects it from freezing in the chilly water in which it spends most of its life, is represented in this platypus toy by thick woolly chenille yarn.

How easy is it to make?

Easy! The only shaping is very minimal, and all the limbs are knitted from the same pattern.

Needles: 3¼mm (size 10, US 3)

Yarn: 50g DK chenille in black; 20g chunky yarn in mid brown; 20g DK in chestnut brown; scraps of DK in black

Pair 10mm (³/8in) toy safety eyes

Tapestry needle

Washable polyester toy stuffing

Tension

Over st-st, using 3¼mm (size 10, US 3) needles, 26sts and 34 rows to 10cm (4in).

Also . . .

Figures in [square brackets] give the total number of stitches or rows you should have at that stage.

All the information you need to work the Duck-Billed Platypus is in Basic Techniques, p9–13.

BODY AND HEAD
Make one, using black chenille
Cast on 24sts. Working in st-st throughout and beg with a k row, work 2 rows.
Next row: inc one st into first 2sts, k(8), inc one st into next 4sts, k to last 2sts, inc one st into last 2sts. **Next row:** p. Rep last 2 rows, with number of sts in brackets 4 more each time, until you have 56sts total. Work 51 rows; [60 rows total]
Next row: k2 tog, k2 tog, k(20), k2 tog four times, k to last 4sts, k2 tog, k2 tog. **Next row:** p. Rep last 2 rows, with number of sts in brackets 4 less each time, until 24sts rem. **Next row:** p. Cast off.
With smooth sides outwards, fold body and head piece in half. Join end and long side seam. Position and fit toy safety eyes. Fill body and head with stuffing then sew closed.

FEET
Make four, using chestnut
Cast on 20sts. Working in st-st throughout and beg with a k row, work 6 rows.
Next row: inc one st into first st, k8, inc one st into next 2sts, k to last st, inc one st into last st. **Next row:** p. Rep last 2 rows, with number of sts in brackets 2 more each time, until you have 32sts total. Work 9 rows; [20 rows total]. Cast off.

With smooth sides outwards, fold foot piece in half. Join cast off edge and side seam, fill with stuffing then sew closed. Ladderstitch to body. With black yarn, sew lines of stitches to represent webbed feet (see diagram below).

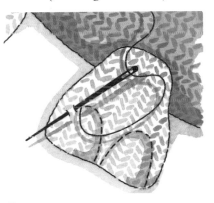

BILL

Make one, using mid brown
Cast on 24sts. **First row:** k11, p2, k11. **Next row:** p11, k2, p11. Rep last 2 rows until 18 rows total have been worked.
Next row: k2 tog, k2 tog, k4, k2 tog four times, k4, k2 tog, k2 tog; [16sts]. **Next k row:** (k2 tog, k4, k2 tog) twice; [12sts]. **Next row:** p. Cast off.
With smooth sides outwards, fold bill piece in half. Join around shaped edge and fill with stuffing. Sew open end to front of body, just under eyes.

TAIL

Make one, using mid brown

Cast on 30sts. Working in st-st throughout and beg with a k row, work 30 rows.

Next row: k2 tog, k2 tog, k7, k2 tog four times, k7, k2 tog, k2 tog; [22sts]. **Next k row:** k2 tog, k2 tog, k3, k2 tog four times, k3, k2 tog, k2 tog; [14sts]. **Next row:** p. Cast off.

With smooth sides outwards, fold tail piece in half. Join around shaped edge, fill with stuffing then sew closed. Ladderstitch to back of body.

CHEEKS

Make two, using mid brown

Cast on 12sts. Beg with a k row, st-st 6 rows. Cast off.

Sew cheek on one side of beak, leaving middle slightly puffy to make it stand out (see picture below as guide).

NOSE RIDGE

Make one, using mid brown

Cast on 8sts. Beg with a k row, st-st 4 rows.

Next row: k2 tog, k4, k2 tog. **Next row:** p. Cast off.

Sew nose ridge at top of beak, between eyes, leaving middle slightly puffy to make it stand out.

MOUTH

With black yarn, sew lines around edge of beak (see picture below as guide).

WOMBAT

Approximate size: 17.5cm (7in)

A fat, bear-like creature, the wombat has a thick heavy body, small eyes, a massive flattened head and a characteristic shambling walk. So, like many of their other marsupial cousins in Australia, wombats are very slow moving and can appear quite dopey. Everything they do – be it digging with their powerful front paws for tasty roots, or burrowing to find shade from the hot Outback sun – is carried out slowly and laboriously. Everything is geared towards saving energy, since food and water are hard to find, and nothing can be wasted.

The coarse coat, which also helps the wombat to keep warm and store up its energy, has been mimicked in this toy by using a textured yarn which has a dark thread running through it to make the wombat look more hairy.

How easy is it to make?

Easy! It's all knitted in one colour, and is small and quick to knit.

Needles: 3 1/4mm (size 10, US 3)

Yarn: 40g DK in brown; scraps of DK in black

Pair 10mm (3/8in) toy safety eyes

Tapestry and sewing needles

Black thread

Washable polyester toy stuffing

Tension

Over st-st, using 3 1/4mm (size 10, US 3) needles, 26sts and 34 rows to 10cm (4in).

Also . . .

Figures in [square brackets] give the total number of stitches or rows you should have at that stage.

All the information you need to work the Wombat is in Basic Techniques, p9–13.

BODY AND HEAD
Make one, using brown
Cast on 14sts. Working in st-st throughout, and beg with a k row, work 2 rows.
Next row: inc one st into first 2sts, k(3), inc one st into next 4sts, k to last 2sts, inc one st into last 2sts. **Next row:** p. Rep last 2 rows, with number of sts in brackets 4 more each time, until you have 46sts total. Work 39 rows; [48 rows total].

Next row: (k3, inc one st into next st) five times, k6, (inc one st into next st, k3) five times; [56sts]. **Next k row:** (k3, inc one st into next 2sts) five times, k6, (inc one st into next 2sts, k3) five times; [76sts]. **Next k row:** k4, (inc one st into next 2sts, k5) four times, inc one st into next 2sts, k8, inc one st into next 2sts, (k5, inc one st into next 2sts) four times, k4; [96sts]. Work 5 rows; [58 rows total].
Next row: k2, (k2 tog, k4) fifteen times, k2 tog, k2; [80sts]. **Next k row:** k4, (k2 tog, k3) fourteen times, k2 tog, k4; [65sts]. **Next k row:** k4, (k2 tog, k2) fourteen times, k2 tog, k3; [50sts].
Next k row: k3, (k2 tog, k1) fourteen times, k2 tog, k3; [35sts]. **Next k row:** k1, k2 tog seventeen times; [18sts].
Next k row: k2 tog nine times; [9sts]. **Next row:** p. Break off yarn, slip end through rem sts and pull tight. This is the nose end.
With smooth sides outwards and starting from nose end, join long side seam. Position and fit toy safety eyes. Fill with stuffing then sew closed.

LEGS
Make four, using brown
Cast on 20sts. Beg with a k row, st-st 18 rows. Cast off.
With smooth sides outwards, fold leg piece in half. Join along bottom and side seams, fill with stuffing then sew closed. Ladderstitch to body.

EARS
Make two, using brown
Cast on 18sts. Beg with a k row, st-st 6 rows.
Next row: k2 tog, k5, k2 tog, k2 tog, k5, k2 tog. **Next row:** p. Cast off.
With smooth sides outwards, fold ear piece in half. Join around edge, then ladderstitch to head.

TAIL
Make one, using brown.
Cast on 10sts. (Edge to be joined to body.) Working in st-st throughout and beg with a k row, work 4 rows.
K2 tog at both ends of next and every foll k row until 2sts rem. **Next row:** p2 tog. Break off yarn, slip end through rem st and pull tight. Hide end of yarn by sewing it back through the knitting.
With smooth side outwards, sew long straight edge of tail to body.

NOSE
Make one, using dark brown
Cast on 6sts. P 1 row. Working in st-st throughout, next row: inc one st into first st, k4, inc one st into last st.
Work 3 rows. **Next row:** k2 tog, k4, k2 tog. **Next row:** p. Cast off.
Sew nose to front of face.

MOUTH AND NOSTRILS
With black yarn, sew one big stitch under nose for a mouth. Secure yarn in a smooth curve with tiny stitches worked in black thread (see Basic Techniques, p11). Sew two black stitches at base of nose for nostrils.

KANGAROO

Approximate sizes: Mother 38cm (15in) excluding tail; Joey 11.5cm (4 3/4 in)

When kangaroos are born, they're so small that their mother hardly notices that they've arrived. Safe inside the pouch the baby, called a Joey, grows and grows, feeding on its mother's milk. And when it's old enough to leave the pouch and eat plants . . . it stays in the pouch and grows some more! The poor mothers are often seen waddling around with their huge teenage offspring folded up and wedged into their bulging pouch. As the mother bends over to eat, so the Joey leans nonchalantly out from its cosy cradle and nibbles a little greenery.

This little Joey hasn't got too big just yet – it still doesn't have the huge muscular legs of its parents to send it bounding across the Australian Outback, so it's still welcome in its mother's huge pocket.

How easy is it to make?

Straightforward. All the shaping is very easy, but the kangaroo is quite big, which might make it daunting for a beginner's project. Why not start with a baby Joey and work your way up from there?

For both kangaroos

Needles: 3 1/4mm (size 10, US 3)

Tapestry and sewing needles

Black thread

Washable polyester toy stuffing

For the mother kangaroo

Yarn: 80g chunky yarn in mid brown; scraps of DK in black

(One 150g ball of chunky yarn is enough for a mother and baby kangaroo)

Pair 14mm (1/2 in) toy safety eyes

For the baby Joey

Yarn: 20g chunky yarn in mid brown; scraps of DK in black

Pair 10mm (3/8 in) toy safety eyes

Tension

Over st-st, using 3 1/4mm (size 10, US 3) needles, 22sts and 30 rows to 10cm (4in).

Also . . .

Figures in [square brackets] give the total number of stitches or rows you should have at that stage.

All the information you need to work the Kangaroo and Joey is in Basic Techniques, p9–13.

MOTHER

BODY AND HEAD
Make one, using mid brown
Cast on 12sts. This is the nose end. Working in st-st throughout and beg with a k row, work 2 rows.
Next row: inc one st into first st, k(4), inc one st into next 2sts, k to last st, inc one st into last st. Work 3 rows. Rep last 4 rows, with number of sts in brackets 2 more each time, until you have 32sts total. Work 29 rows; [48 rows total].
Next row: k(5), inc one st into next st, k20, inc one st into next st, k to end of row. **Next row:** p. Rep last 2 rows, with number of sts in brackets 1 more each time, until you have 42sts total.

Next k row: k8, inc one st into next st, k to last 9sts, inc one st into next st, k8. Work 3 rows. Rep last 4 rows until you have 58sts total. Work 9 rows; [96 rows total].
Next row: (k2 tog, k25, k2 tog) twice; [54sts]. **Next k row:** k2 tog, k5, k2 tog, k(16), k2 tog, k2 tog, k to last 9sts, k2 tog, k5, k2 tog. **Next row:** p. Rep last 2 rows, with number of sts in brackets 3 less each time, until 30sts rem.
Next k row: (k2 tog, k2 tog, k1) twice, k1, k2 tog four times, k1, (k1, k2 tog, k2 tog) twice; [18sts]. **Next row:** p. Cast off.
With smooth sides outwards, fold body and head piece in half. Join nose end and long straight seam (running down front of kangaroo). Position and fit toy safety eyes. Fill with stuffing and sew closed.
Head: Approx 10cm (4in) from end of nose, bend head down at right angles to body (see Basic Techniques, p11) and ladderstitch in position.

TAIL
Make one, using mid brown
Cast on 40sts. Working in st-st throughout and beg with a k row, work 4 rows.

Next row: k18, k2 tog, k2 tog, k to end of row; [38sts]. **Next k row:** k17, k2 tog, k2 tog, k to end of row; [36sts].

Next k row: k(16), k2 tog, k2 tog, k to end of row. Work 3 rows. Rep last 4 rows, with number of sts in brackets 1 less each time, until 10sts rem. Work 3 rows.

Next row: (k2 tog, k1, k2 tog) twice; [6sts]. **Next row:** p. Cast off.

With smooth sides outwards, fold tail piece in half. Join narrow end and long side seam, and fill with stuffing. Sew open end to back of kangaroo, pointing slightly downwards.

LEGS

Make two, using mid brown
Cast on 24sts. This is the top of the hip. Working in st-st throughout and beg with a k row, work 2 rows.

Next row: inc one st into first st, k(10), inc one st into next 2sts, k to last st, inc one st into last st. **Next row:** p. Rep last 2 rows, with number of sts in brackets 2 more each time, until you have 36sts total. Work 13 rows; [20 rows total].

Next row: (k2 tog, k14, k2 tog) twice; [32sts]. **Next k row:** (k2 tog, k12, k2 tog) twice; [28sts]. **Next k row:** (k2 tog, k10, k2 tog) twice; [24sts].

Making the foot: Next k row: Cast off 6sts, k to end of row. **Next row:** cast off 6sts, p to end of row; [12sts].

Cont on rem 12sts, work 28 rows. **Next row:** (k2 tog, k2) three times; [9sts]. **Next k row:** (k2 tog, k1) three times; [6sts]. **Next row:** p. Cast off.

With smooth sides outwards, fold leg piece in half. Join seam around fat hip section and fill with stuffing. Join seam along narrow foot section, fill with stuffing then sew closed.

Bend foot up at right angles towards hip and ladderstitch in position (see picture as guide). Ladderstitch leg to side of body.

ARMS

Make two, using mid brown
Cast on 16sts. Working in st-st throughout and beg with a k row, work 2 rows.

K2 tog at both ends of next 2 k rows; [12sts]. Work 23 rows; [28 rows total]. K2 tog at both ends of next and every foll k row until 4sts rem. **Next row:** p. Cast off.

With smooth sides outwards, fold arm piece in half. Join long straight seam, fill with stuffing then sew closed. Bend arm to form elbow and ladderstitch in position. Rep for wrist. Ladderstitch arm to side of body.

EARS

Make two, using mid brown
Cast on 8sts. Working in st-st throughout and beg with a k row, work 12 rows.

K2 tog at both ends of next and every foll k row until 2sts rem. Break off yarn, slip end through rem sts and pull tight. Hide end of yarn by sewing it back through knitting.

With smooth sides outwards, fold ear piece in half and sew base to side of head. Make extra stitches to hold ear upright against side of head.

POUCH

Make one, using mid brown
Cast on 24sts. This is the top of the pouch. Working in st-st throughout and beg with a k row, work 20 rows.

Next row: k2 tog, k6, k2 tog, k4, k2 tog, k6, k2 tog; [20sts]. **Next k row:** (k2 tog, k4) three times, k2 tog; [16sts]. **Next k row:** (k2 tog, k2) twice, (k2, k2 tog) twice; [12sts]. **Next row:** p. Cast off.

Pin pouch to front of kangaroo, leaving front puffy to allow room for baby. Sew sides and bottom in position. Remove pins. Work a line of running stitch (see Basic Techniques, p11) close to top edge of pouch and pull gently to straighten edge of pouch. Secure yarn and hide end by making a few stitches.

JOEY

BODY, HEAD AND TAIL

Make one, using mid brown
Cast on 10sts. This is the nose end. P 1 row. Working in st-st throughout, next row: inc one st into first st, k3, inc one st into next 2sts, k3, inc one st into last st; [14sts]. Work 35 rows; [37 rows total].

K2 tog at both ends of next and every foll alt k row until 6sts rem. **Next k row:** k2 tog three times. Break off yarn, slip end through rem sts and pull tight.

With smooth sides outwards, fold body, head and tail piece in half. Join nose end and long straight seam. Position and fit toy safety eyes. Fill with stuffing and sew closed. About 5cm (2in) from rounded nose end, bend head down at right angle to body and ladderstitch in position. About 7.5cm (3in) from pointed end of tail, bend tail up at right angle to body and ladderstitch in position.

ARMS AND LEGS

Make four, using mid brown
Cast on 6sts. Working in st-st throughout and beg with a k row, work 10 rows.

Next row: k2 tog, k2, k2 tog; [4sts]. **Next k row:** k2 tog, k2 tog; [2sts]. Break off yarn, slip end through rem sts and pull tight.

With smooth sides outwards, fold limb piece in half. Join side seam, fill with stuffing and sew closed. Ladderstitch to body.

EARS

Make two, using mid brown

Cast on 5sts. Working in st-st throughout and beg with a k row, work 6 rows.

Next row: k2 tog, k1, k2 tog. **Next row:** p. **Next row:** k3 tog. Break off yarn, slip end through rem st and pull tight. Hide end of yarn by sewing it back through knitting.

Fold ear piece in half and sew base to side of head.

Finishing mother and Joey kangaroos

MOUTH AND NOSTRILS

With black yarn, sew two or three stitches on either side of nose for nostrils. Use long straight stitches to make a mouth. Secure yarn in a smooth curve with tiny stitches worked in black thread (see Basic Techniques, p11, and picture as guides).

VARIATIONS

The adult kangaroo shown here is a mother, with a pouch for her baby. For a father kangaroo, simply use the same instructions but leave out the pouch.

DOWN ON THE FARM

FARMER

Approximate size: 29cm (11½in)

Farming is one of the most important professions in the world. Whatever they grow, be it plants or animals, farmers help to provide things that make our lives possible – essentials like food and clothing, but also fun things like the wool for all these toys! Farmers often take a great pride in the care of their land and stock, handing on their wealth of knowledge and experience through their children and keeping tradition alive. And they take a particular pride in taking good care of their animals.

This farmer has a big workload, with chickens, pigs, a duck and even a Highland bull to look after – they should certainly keep her very busy!

How easy is it to make?

Straightforward. The pieces aren't complicated. There's some colour-changing, and the hair may take a little extra time to complete.

Needles: 3¼mm (size 10, US 3)

Yarn: 50g DK in skin colour; 40g DK in green; 20g each DK in fawn and pale yellow; scraps of DK in black, dark brown, white, bright yellow and dark blue

Pair 10mm (3/8in) toy safety eyes

Tapestry and sewing needles

Dark brown thread

Washable polyester toy stuffing

Props: miniature basket; modelling clay for eggs; remnant of checked fabric to line basket

---

Tension

Over st-st, using 3¼mm (size 10, US 3) needles, 26sts and 34 rows to 10cm (4in).

Also . . .

Figures in [square brackets] give the total number of stitches or rows you should have at that stage.

The Basic Person Pattern is on p12.

All the information you need to work the Farmer is in Basic Techniques, p9–13.

BODY AND HEAD
Make one, using green, fawn and skin colour
Cast on 44sts in green. Beg with a k row, st-st 12 rows. Next row: p16, k12, p16. **Next row:** p.
Change to fawn and beg with a k row, st-st 14 rows. Work as for Basic Person pattern from 'Shape shoulder' to 'Shape chin'.
Change to skin colour, work as for Basic Person Pattern from 'Shape chin' to end.

LEGS
Make two, using black and green
Work as for Basic Person Pattern using following colours: work first 22 rows in black; rem rows in green.
Make up as for Basic Person Pattern and ladderstitch to body.

ARMS
Make two, using skin colour and fawn
Cast on 14sts in skin colour. P 1 row. Working in st-st throughout, next row: inc one st into first st, k5, inc one st into next 2sts, k to last st, inc one st into last st; [18sts]. Work 22 rows; [24 rows total].
Change to fawn. K 3 rows. This will form ridge round edge of sleeve.
Working in st-st, k2 tog at both ends and near middle of next and every foll k row until 3sts rem. Cast off.
Make up as for Basic Person Pattern and ladderstitch to body.

EARS
Make two, using skin colour
Work and attach as for Basic Person Pattern.

DUNGAREES FRONT PANEL
Make one, using green
Cast on 12sts. Beg with a k row, st-st 14 rows. Cast off.
Sew front panel to body, with bottom edge aligned to top of trousers (see picture as guide).
Embroider white lazy daisy on front panel (see Basic Techniques, p11), with a few extra stitches in bright yellow at the centre.
Straps: Make a 12.5cm (5in) single chain of green yarn. Sew one end to top corner of dungarees front panel, take it over farmer's shoulder and to opposite side of body. Sew end to top of green trousers. Rep for second strap.

MOUTH
Work as for Basic Person Pattern, using dark brown.

HAIR
Work top of hair as for Basic Person Pattern, in pale yellow, and make plaits to match. Make hair ties in dark blue.

FINISHING TOUCHES
If you're going to make chickens for your farmer to look after, line a miniature basket with fabric. Make tiny eggs with modelling clay – you could even paint them so that the farmer can choose between white and speckled eggs for her breakfast.

HIGHLAND BULL

Approximate size: 33cm (13in)

Highland bulls are majestic animals with a bearing and presence that makes them look almost regal. With their great sweeping horns, they hold their heads proudly, inviting admiration and respect. Only in the rain do they look anything less than magnificent, when their shaggy coat can become bedraggled. So be warned – if you want to wash your knitted highland bull, make sure you have a brush handy to fluff out his fringe once he's dried!

How easy is it to make?

Easy! The shaping is very simple, with just a small amount of colour-changing. If you find fluffy yarn hard to manage, or if you're knitting this toy for a baby, substitute ginger DK yarn for the mohair.

Tension

Over st-st, using 3¾mm (size 9, US 4) needles, 18sts and 28 rows to 10cm (4in).

Also . . .

Figures in [square brackets] give the total number of stitches or rows you should have at that stage.

All the information you need to work the Highland Bull is in Basic Techniques, p9–13.

Needles: *3¾mm (size 9, US 4)*

Yarn: *60g DK in ginger mohair; 20g DK in mid brown; scraps of DK in pale brown and black*

Pair 14mm (¹/₂ in) toy safety eyes

Tapestry and sewing needles

Black thread

Washable polyester toy stuffing

BODY
Make one, using ginger mohair
Cast on 30sts. Working in st-st throughout and beg with a k row, work 2 rows.
Next row: inc one st into first 2sts, k(11), inc one st into next 4sts, k to last 2sts, inc one st into last 2sts. **Next row:** p. Rep last 2 rows, with number of sts in brackets 4 more each time, until you have 54sts total. **Next k row:** inc one st into first st, k25, inc one st into next 2sts, k to last st, inc one st into last st; [58sts]. Work 47 rows; [56 rows total].
K or P2 tog at both ends of next and every foll row until 30sts rem. **Next k row:** (k2 tog, k11, k2 tog) twice; [26sts]. **Next row:** p. Cast off. This is the neck end.
With smooth sides together, fold body piece in half. Join neck end and side seams, fill with stuffing then sew closed.

FACE
Make one, using ginger mohair and mid brown DK
Cast on 36sts in ginger mohair. Working in st-st throughout and beg with a k row, work 2 rows. K2 tog at both ends of next and every foll alt k row until 26sts rem. Work 3 rows; [22 rows total].
Change to mid brown yarn, work 6 rows. **Next row:** k5,

k2 tog, k2 tog, k8, k2 tog, k2 tog, k to end of row; [22sts].
Next k row: k4, k2 tog, k2 tog, k6, k2 tog, k2 tog, k to end of row; [18sts]. **Next row:** p. Cast off. This is the nose end.
With smooth sides outwards, fold face piece in half. Join nose end and side seams. Position and fit toy safety eyes. Fill with stuffing, then sew open end to neck end of body (see picture as guide).

LEGS
Make four, using ginger mohair and mid brown
Cast on 24sts in ginger mohair. Working in st-st throughout and beg with a k row, work 8 rows.
Change to mid brown, work 6 rows. K2 tog at both ends of next and every foll k row until 16sts rem. Work 3 rows. Cast off. This is the foot end.
With smooth sides outwards, fold leg piece in half. Join narrow end and side seams, fill with stuffing and sew closed. Ladderstitch to body. Sew across leg along line where colours meet.

HORNS
Make two, using pale brown
Cast on 12sts. Working in st-st throughout and beg with a k row, work 12 rows.
Next row: k2 tog, k3, inc one st

into next 2sts, k to last 2sts, k2 tog; [12sts]. **Next row:** p. Rep last 2 rows twice more; [18 rows total].

K2 tog at both ends of next and every foll k row until 2sts rem. Break off yarn, slip end through rem sts and pull tight.

With smooth sides outwards, fold horn piece in half and join along side seam. Fill with stuffing, then sew open end to side of head (see picture as guide).

EARS

Make two, using ginger mohair

Cast on 12sts. Working in st-st throughout and beg with a k row, work 14 rows.

K2 tog at both ends of next and every foll k row until 2sts rem. Break off yarn, slip end through rem sts and pull tight. Hide end of yarn by sewing it back through knitting.

Fold ear piece in half and sew to head just under base of horn.

FRINGE

Where top of face joins body, sew a loop of ginger mohair yarn, about 5cm (2in) long, to hang down over face. Secure base of loop with a few sts. Rep all along top of face. Cut loose ends of loops to make a fringe. Trim ends of fringe to give neat edge.

TAIL

Cut six 25cm (10in) lengths of ginger mohair. Holding lengths in a bunch, tie in middle with another piece of ginger yarn (use this later to attach tail). Fold lengths of yarn in half and divide ends into three groups of four. Plait groups together (see Basic Techniques, p11) until 2.5cm (1in) from end. Tie end of plait in knot. Sew tail to back of body.

MOUTH AND NOSTRILS

With black yarn, make two or three stitches on either side of nose as nostrils. Use long straight stitches to make a mouth. Secure yarn in a smooth curve with tiny stitches worked in black thread (see Basic Techniques, p11, and picture as guides).

PIGS AND PIGLETS

Approximate sizes: Adults 20cm (8in); Piglets 12.5cm (5in)

Pigs are well known for loving food, and these tubby little pigs have stomachs to show that they deserve the reputation! Pigs also love to snuffle about in the mud to detect roots and vegetables with their sensitive noses. Sometimes, for this reason, pigs are kept as 'truffle hounds' for sniffing out the rare fungal delicacy growing among the roots of oak trees. It is a tradition that has gone on for centuries, and in this knitted farmyard live the distant cousins of those historic truffle hunters. The four different designs of pig you can choose from are all based on the markings and colours of traditional breeds.

How easy is it to make?

Easy! The pigs and piglets that are made in a single colour are simple to knit. The Saddleback pigs are only slightly more complex, with a change of colour on their bodies. The Gloucester Old Spot pigs and piglets may prove a bit more challenging with their embroidered spots.

Tension

Over st-st, using 3 1/4mm (size 10, US 3) needles, 26sts and 34 rows to 10cm (4in).

Also . . .

Figures in [square brackets] give the total number of stitches or rows you should have at that stage.

All the information you need to work the Pigs and Piglets is in Basic Techniques, p9–13.

Needles: 3 ¼mm (size 10, US 3)

Scraps of DK yarn in dark brown

Pair 10mm (³/₈ in) toy safety eyes

Tapestry needle

Washable polyester toy stuffing

Yarn for pigs: *Large White pig: 40g DK in pale brown; Saddleback pig: 40g DK in black; 20g DK in pink; Gloucester Old Spot pig: 40g DK in pink; scraps of DK in brown; Tamworth pig: 40g DK in ginger*

Yarn for piglets: *Large White piglet: 20g DK in pale brown; Saddleback piglet: 20g DK in black; 10g DK in pink; Gloucester Old Spot piglet: 20g DK in pink; scraps of DK in brown; Tamworth piglet: 20g DK in ginger*

Note: One 50g ball of DK is enough to make a pig and piglet

ADULT PIG

The following instructions are for an adult pig of the Large White breed. Colour variations for other pig breeds are included at the end.

BODY AND HEAD
Make one, using pale brown

Cast on 24sts. Working in st-st throughout and beg with a k row, work 2 rows.

Next k row: inc one st into first 2sts, k8, inc one st into next 4sts, k8, inc one st into last 2sts; [32sts].

Next k row: inc one st into first st, k(14), inc one st into next 2sts, k to last st, inc one st into last st. **Next row:** p. Rep last 2 rows, with number of sts in brackets 2 more each time, until you have 44sts total. Work 39 rows; [48 rows total].

Next row: (k2 tog, k18, k2 tog) twice; [40sts]. **Next k row:** (k2 tog, k16, k2 tog) twice; [36sts]. **Next k row:** (k2 tog, k14, k2 tog) twice; [32sts]. **Next k row:** (k2 tog, k2 tog, k1, k2 tog, k2, k2 tog, k1, k2 tog, k2 tog) twice; [20sts]. **Next row:** (p2 tog, p6, p2 tog) twice; [16sts]. Work 8 rows; [64 rows total]. Cast off. This is the snout end.

With smooth sides outwards, fold body and head piece in half and join long side seam. Position and fit toy safety eyes. Fill with stuffing and sew back end closed, leaving snout end open.

SNOUT
Make one, using pale brown

Cast on 8sts. P 1 row. **Next row:** inc one st into first st, k6, inc one st into last st; [10sts]. Work 3 rows; [5 rows total]. **Next row:** k2 tog, k6, k2 tog; [8sts]. **Next row:** p. Cast off.

Cover snout hole in head with snout piece and sew in position.

FRONT LEGS

Make two, using pale brown

Cast on 12sts. Working in st-st throughout and beg with a k row, work 8 rows.

Next row: inc one st into first st, k4, inc one st into next 2sts, k4, inc one st into last st; [16sts]. Work 3 rows; [12 rows total].

Next row: inc one st into first st, k6, inc one st into next 2sts, k6, inc one st into last st; [20sts]* Work 5 rows; [18 rows total].

#Next row: (k2 tog, k6, k2 tog) twice; [16sts]. **Next k row:** (k2 tog, k4, k2 tog) twice; [12sts]. **Next row:** p. Cast off.

With smooth sides outwards, fold leg piece in half. Join narrow end and side seam, fill with stuffing and sew closed. Sew a 2.5cm (1in) line of stitches up centre of foot, at right angles to base of foot, forming trotter. Ladderstitch leg to body.

BACK LEGS

Make two, using pale brown

Work as for front leg to *. Work 7 rows; [20 rows total]. Work as for front leg from # to end.

Make up back leg as for front leg (above) and ladderstitch to body.

EARS

Make two, using pale brown

Cast on 8sts. Working in st-st throughout and beg with a k row, work 10 rows.

K2 tog at both ends of next and every foll k row until 2sts rem. **Next row:** p. **Next row:** k2 tog. Break off yarn, slip end through rem st and pull tight. Hide end of yarn by sewing it back through knitting.

Sew straight edge of ear to head (see picture on p55 as guide).

PIGLET

The following instructions are for a piglet of the Large White breed. Colour variations for other piglet breeds are included at the end.

BODY AND HEAD

Make one, using pale brown

Cast on 16sts. Working in st-st throughout and beg with a k row, work 2 rows.

Next row: inc one st into first 2sts, k4, inc one st into next 4sts, k4, inc one st into last 2sts; [24sts]. **Next k row:** inc one st into first st, k10, inc one st into next 2sts, k10, inc one st into last st; [28sts]. Work 25 rows; [30 rows total].

Next row: (k2 tog, k10, k2 tog) twice; [24sts]. **Next k row:** (k2 tog, k3, k2 tog, k3, k2 tog) twice; [18sts]. **Next row:** (p2 tog, p5, p2 tog) twice; [14sts]. Work 6 rows; [40 rows total]. Cast off. This is the snout end.

Make up as for adult pig body and head.

SNOUT

Make one, using pale brown

Cast on 5sts. P 1 row. Working in st-st throughout, next row: inc one st into first st, k3, inc one st into last st; [7sts]. Work 3 rows; [5 rows total].

Next row: k2 tog, k3, k2 tog; [5sts]. **Next row:** p. Cast off. Attach snout as for adult pig.

FRONT LEGS

Make two, using pale brown

Cast on 8sts. Working in st-st throughout and beg with a k row, work 6 rows.

Next row: inc one st into first st, k2, inc one st into next 2sts, k2, inc one st into last st; [12sts].* Work 5 rows; [12 rows total]. **Next row:** (k2 tog, k2, k2 tog) twice; [8sts]. **Next row:** p. Cast off.

Make up as for adult pig leg and ladderstitch to body.

BACK LEGS

Make two, using pale brown

Work as for front leg to *. Work 3 rows; [10 rows total]. **Next row:** inc one st into first st, k4, inc one st into next 2sts, k4, inc one st into last st; [16sts]. Work 5 rows; [16 rows total]. **Next row:** (k2 tog, k4, k2 tog) twice; [12sts]. **Next row:** (p2 tog, p2, p2 tog) twice; [8sts]. Cast off.

Make up as for adult pig leg and ladderstitch to body.

EARS

Make two, using pale brown

Cast on 6sts. Working in st-st throughout and beg with a k row, work 6 rows.

Next row: k2 tog, k2, k2 tog; [4sts]. **Next row:** p. **Next row:** k2 tog, k2 tog; [2sts]. **Next row:** p2 tog. Break off yarn, slip end through rem st and pull tight. Hide end of yarn by sewing it back through knitting.

Sew straight edge of ear to head.

Finishing pig and piglet

TAIL

For an adult pig, make a 7.5cm (3in) length of single chain in pale brown yarn (see Basic Techniques, p10). For a baby pig, make a 5cm (2in) chain. At one end of chain, hide end of yarn by sewing it back along chain, and make a stitch to hold chain in characteristic curly loop. Sew other end of chain in position on pig's back.

NOSTRILS AND MOUTH

With dark brown yarn, make two or three stitches on either side of snout as nostrils. Use long straight stitches for a mouth (see Basic Techniques, p11, and picture opposite as guides).

COLOUR VARIATIONS

Saddleback pig or piglet, follow pig or piglet instructions, using the following colours: make front legs in pink; make back legs, snout, ears and tail in black. Make Saddleback pig's body and head as follows: work first 28 rows of the body and head piece in black, the next 10 rows in pink; rem rows in black. Make Saddleback piglet's body and head as follows: work first 18 rows of body and head piece in black, next 7 rows in pink, rem rows in black.

Gloucester Old Spot pig or piglet, follow the pig or piglet instructions. Make all pieces in pink. Using dark brown yarn, make spots on pig's back with Swiss darning (see Basic Techniques, p11, picture and charts, right).

Tamworth pig or piglet, follow pig or piglet instructions. Make all pieces in ginger.

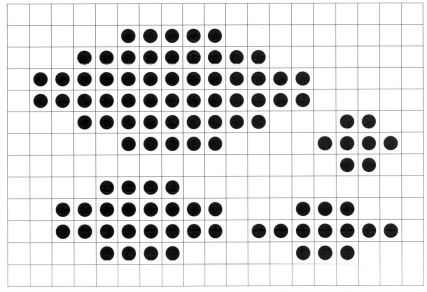

Swiss darning stitch guide for spots for adult Gloucester Old Spot pig

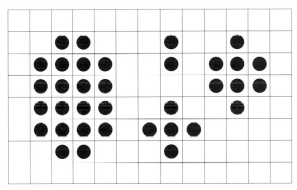

Swiss darning stitch guide for spots for Gloucester Old Spot piglet

Cat

Approximate size: 13cm (5in)

When farm cats get inside the farmhouse, they're as friendly and cuddly as anything, purring round the farmer's feet to persuade her to give them some cream. But outside in the farmyard, they are tough and wily, keeping an eye on the rats and mice that infest the barns. Cats always seem to have this double personality – maintaining an aloof independence by day, and becoming wild and unruly at night.

These little farm cats definitely have a twinkle in their eye, and share this double life. They look fluffy and sweet, but remain alert in case they might catch a mouse unawares.

How easy is it to make?

Challenging. The shapes of the pieces are easy, but working in stripes can become confusing for a beginner. Making up the body and gusset might also prove a bit fiddly. If you're not confident, try knitting the striped pieces of the cat in a single plain colour instead. If you find fluffy yarn hard to manage, or if you're knitting this toy for a baby, substitute smooth DK yarn for the mohair.

Needles: Size 9 (3³/₄mm, US 4)

Scraps of green felt

Tapestry and sewing needles

Thread in black and green

Washable polyester toy stuffing

Yarn for a ginger tom: Small amounts (less than 10g) DK mohair in ginger (colour A), orange (colour B), yellow (colour C) and white; scraps of DK in black

Yarn for a tabby cat: Small amounts (less than 10g) DK mohair in dark grey (colour A), mid grey (colour B) and white (colour C); scraps of DK in black

Tension

Over st-st, using size 9 (3 ¹/₄mm, US 4) needles, 18sts and 28 rows to 10cm (4in).

Also . . .

Figures in [square brackets] give the total number of stitches or rows you should have at that stage.

All the information you need to work the Cats is in Basic Techniques, p9–13.

The following instructions are for the ginger tom. To make a tabby cat, follow the same instructions, but substitute the tabby colours.

BODY AND HEAD

Make one, using stripes of ginger (A), orange (B) and yellow (C) mohair

Throughout this piece, work stripes of two rows of each colour in sequence: A, B and C (see Basic Techniques, p10).

Cast on 20sts in colour A. Working in st-st throughout and beg with a k row, work 16 rows.

Next row: inc one st into first st, k7, k2 tog, k2 tog, k to last st, inc one st into last st; [20sts]. **Next row:** p. Rep last two rows twice more; [22 rows total]. Mark both ends of last row with coloured markers.

Next row: inc one st into first 2sts, k6, inc one st into next 4sts, k to last 2sts, inc one st into last 2sts; [28sts]. **Next k row:** inc one st into first 2sts, k10, inc one st into next 4sts, k to last 2sts, inc one st into last 2sts; [36sts]. Work 5 rows; [30 rows total].

Next row: (k2 tog, k2 tog, k10, k2 tog, k2 tog) twice; [28sts]. **Next k row:** (k2 tog, k2 tog, k6, k2 tog, k2 tog) twice; [20sts]. **Next row:** p. Cast off.

With smooth sides outwards, fold body piece in half, matching up coloured markers. Join seam between top of head and markers, using colour B.

STOMACH

Make one, using white mohair

Cast on 3sts. Working in st-st throughout and beg with a k row, work 2 rows.

Inc one st at both ends of next and every foll k row until you have 11sts total. Work 13 rows; [22 rows total]. K2 tog at both ends of next and every foll alt k row until 3sts rem. Work 3 rows. **Next row:** k3 tog. Break off yarn, slip end through rem st and pull tight. This is the neck end.

With smooth sides outwards, match up pointed neck end of stomach piece with coloured marker on body piece. Using white yarn, join side of stomach piece down front of body and along base to second point of stomach piece. Fill cat with stuffing, then join second side of stomach to open edge of body. Remove markers.

FRONT LEGS

Make two, using white, ginger (A), orange (B) and yellow (C) mohair

Cast on 4sts in white. P 1 row. Working in st-st throughout, next row: inc one st into each st; [8sts].

Work 3 rows.* Work 16 rows in two-row stripes of A, B and C (2 rows of each colour in sequence). Cast off.

With smooth sides outwards, fold leg piece in half. Join side seam with colour B (use white for paw section). Fill with stuffing and ladderstitch to front of body.

Bend white paw up at right angle to leg and ladderstitch in position (see diagram on p11 as guide).

BACK LEGS

Make two, using white, ginger (A), orange (B) and yellow (C) mohair

Work as for front legs to *. Work 10 rows in two-row stripes of A, B and C (2 rows of each colour in sequence). Cast off.

Make up back leg as for front leg (above), but do not make a paw. Ladderstitch leg to side of body (see picture as guide).

TAIL

Make one, using ginger (A), orange (B) and yellow (C) mohair

Cast on 8sts. Working in st-st throughout and beg with a k row, work 26 rows in two-row stripes of A, B and C. Cont in final colour, next row: k2 tog four times. Break off yarn, slip end through rem sts and pull tight.

With smooth sides outwards, fold tail piece in half. Join side seam with colour B and ladderstitch to body.

EAR

Make two, using ginger (A), orange (B) and yellow (C) mohair; two, using white mohair

For striped outer ear: Cast on 6sts in C. Working in st-st throughout and beg with a k row, work 2 rows. Change to B, work 2 rows. Change to A, next row: k2 tog, k2, k2 tog; [4sts]. Cont in A, next k row: k2 tog, k2 tog; [2sts]. **Next k row:** k2 tog. Break off yarn, slip end through rem st and pull tight.

For inner ear: follow instructions for outer ear, but work the whole piece in white.

With smooth sides outwards, match up white ear piece with striped ear piece. With white, join around edge, then ladderstitch ear to head with white side facing forward

FACE

Trace eye pattern piece on to paper and cut it out. Draw round shape twice on green felt and cut out two pieces. With thread, sew eye shapes on to cat's face. With black thread, sew pupils across middle of eyes with straight stitches (see picture on p57 as guide).

Cut two in green

Template for cat's eyes

NOSE AND MOUTH.

With black yarn, make a few stitches in centre of face as a nose. Work an upside down T shape for mouth. Secure yarn in smooth curves with tiny stitches worked in black thread (see Basic Techniques, p11, and picture on p57 as guides).

MALLARD DUCK

Approximate size: 15cm (6in)

When ducklings first hatch out of the egg, they have a natural desire to follow and copy the first creature they set eyes on. This is usually their mother, but sometimes another creature can swing into view at the crucial moment, and the poor confused duckling becomes the faithful friend of the farm dog or cat, or even of the farmer themselves. When this happens, the farmer may have to teach the duck to behave in a duck-like way by showing it how to find the pond, and even wading into the water to encourage the duckling to take its first swim.

This duck's markings are based on the Mallard Duck, with an impressive plumage of bars of different colours. If you'd like to make a female duck of the same species, simply work the following pattern in plain brown.

How easy is it to make?

Straightforward. The head, body and tail are all knitted as a single piece. There's some colour changing to do and, because of its size, making up the duck may be a bit fiddly. If you're making this toy for a small child, sew the eyes from black yarn, and don't make the pipe-cleaner feet. Instead, leave out the feet completely, so the duck will look like it's swimming.

Tension

Over st-st, using 3 1/4mm (size 10, US 3) needles, 26sts and 34 rows to 10cm (4in).

Also . . .

Figures in [square brackets] give the total number of stitches or rows you should have at that stage.

All the information you need to work the Mallard Duck is in Basic Techniques, p9–13.

Needles: 3 1/4mm (size 10, US 3)

Yarn: a small amount (less than 10g each) DK in dark green, chestnut, light brown and black; scraps of DK in white and yellow.

Two small black beads

Two 7.5cm (7in) yellow pipe-cleaners (optional)

Tapestry and sewing needles

Black thread

Washable polyester stuffing

BODY AND HEAD

Make one, using dark green, white, chestnut, light brown and black

Every time you change colour leave long ends of yarn that can be used later to sew up the duck (see Basic Techniques, p10).

Cast on 6sts in dark green. P 1 row. Working in st-st throughout, next row: inc one st into first st, k1, inc one st into next 2sts, k1, inc one st into last st; [10sts].

Next k row: inc one st into first st, k3, inc one st into next 2sts, k3, inc one st into last st; [14sts]. Work 3 rows.

Next k row: k2 tog, k to last 2sts, k2 tog. **Next row:** p. Rep last 2 rows; [10sts]. Work 4 rows; [15 rows total].

Change to white and work 2 rows.

Change to chestnut and work 2 rows. **Next row:** k2, inc one st into next st, k to last 3sts, inc one st into next st, k2. **Next row:** p. Rep last 2 rows until you have 20sts total. **Next row:** p.

Change to light brown. **Next row:** k2, inc one st into next st, k to last 3sts, inc one st into next st, k2. **Next row:** p. Rep last 2 rows until you have 26sts total. Work 13 rows; [18 rows total in light brown or 47 rows total from front of head].

Next row: k2 tog, k2 tog, k to last 4sts, k2 tog, k2 tog. **Next row:** p. Rep last 2 rows.

Change to black. K2 tog at both ends of next and every foll k row until 8sts rem. **Next row:** p. Cast off.

With smooth sides outwards, fold body and head piece in half. Join long side seam, using ends of coloured yarn. Fill with stuffing, then sew closed.

Bend green head down at right angles to neck and ladderstitch in position just above white band (see Basic Techniques, p11).

Bend chestnut neck up at right angles to light brown body and ladderstitch in position.

Bend black tail slightly upwards and ladderstitch in position.

WINGS

Make two, using light brown

Cast on 12sts. Working in st-st throughout and beg with a k row, work 2 rows.

Next row: k2 tog, k to last st, inc one st into last st; [12sts]. **Next row:** p. Rep last two rows until 12 rows total have been worked. Cast off.

Sew straight edge of wing piece to duck with smooth side facing upwards. Hide loose ends of yarn by sewing them back through knitting.

BEAK

Make one, using yellow

Cast on 7sts. Beg with a k row, st-st 6 rows. **Next row:** k2 tog, k1, k2 tog, k2 tog; [4sts]. **Next row:** p. Cast off.

With smooth sides outwards, fold beak piece in half and join side seam. Sew open end to front of head.

EYES

Sew two black beads to sides of face. To finish off, take thread right through duck's head a few times and pull tight to make face narrower, then fasten off securely.

FEET

Wind two pipe-cleaners around each other to make them thicker. As one piece, push pipe-cleaners through duck, from one side to the other. Bend ends of pipe-cleaner down to give two long dangling legs. Bend ends into triangles for feet.

CHICKEN

Approximate sizes: Cockerel 9cm (3 1/2 in); Chicken 7.5cm (3 1/4 in); Chick 6cm (2 1/4 in)

In all cultures all over the world, in every kind of environment, people always keep chickens. They are easy to look after, provide protein-filled eggs almost every day, and are very friendly and cooperative. They can scratch away contentedly in even the poorest of conditions, finding seeds and remnants of food to live on. When you watch a flock of chickens feeding together, it soon becomes apparent that there is a complex social structure, called a 'pecking order'. Each chicken has a fixed place in a complicated hierarchy – chickens higher up the pecking order have a special status, so they get first pick of the food, and strut proudly round their companions enjoying their glory.

The knitted cockerel in this little family of chickens would probably find himself high up the pecking order with his magnificent green and red tail – perfect for showing off to rivals!

How easy is it to make?

Straightforward. To make the texture on each piece, you'll need to work in moss stitch (see Basic Techniques for step-by-step instructions). The chickens are very quick to make, so you may soon find yourself with a whole flock. If you're making this toy for a small child, sew eyes from black thread, and don't make pipe-cleaner feet. Instead, leave out the feet completely, so the chicken looks like it's roosting.

Tension

Over moss st, using 3 1/4 mm (size 10, US 3) needles, 26sts and 34 rows to 10cm (4in).

Also . . .

Figures in [square brackets] give the total number of stitches or rows you should have at that stage.

All the information you need to work the Cockerel, Chicken and Chick is in Basic Techniques, p9–13.

For all chickens

Needles: 3 1/4 mm (size 10, US 3)

Tapestry needle

Washable polyester toy stuffing

For the chicken or cockerel

Yarn: a small amount (less than 10g) DK in chestnut brown; scraps of DK in mid brown and red

Two small black beads

One 17.5cm (7in) yellow pipe-cleaner (optional)

Sewing needle

Black thread

For the cockerel

Scraps of DK yarn in green

For the chick

Yarn: a small amount (less than 10g) DK in yellow; scraps of DK in mid brown and black

One 10cm (4in) yellow pipe-cleaner (optional)

CHICKEN

BODY AND HEAD

Make one, using chestnut brown
Cast on 8sts. Work in moss stitch (see Basic Techniques, p10, for step-by-step instructions for moss stitch) throughout.
Row 1: *k1, p1, rep from * to end of row. **Row 2:** inc one st into first st, (k1, p1) three times, inc one st into last st. **Row 3:** inc one st into first st, (k1, p1) four times, inc one st into last st. **Row 4:** inc one st into first st, (k1, p1) five times, inc one st into last st. **Row 5:** inc one st into first st, (k1, p1) six times, inc one st into last st; [16sts].
Row 6: #p1, k1, rep from # to end of row. **Row 7:** +k1, p1, rep from + to end of row. Rep last two rows four more times; [15 rows total].
Row 16: k2 tog, (p1, k1) six times, p2 tog. **Row 17:** k2 tog, (p1, k1) five times, p2 tog. **Row 18:** k2 tog, (p1, k1) four times, p2 tog. **Row 19:** k2 tog, (p1, k1) three times, p2 tog; [8sts].

Row 20: rep row 6. **Row 21:** rep row 7. **Row 22:** rep row 6. **Row 23:** rep row 7. **Row 24:** rep row 6. **Row 25:** (k2 tog, p2 tog) twice. **Row 26:** (p1, k1) twice. Cast off. This is the head end.

Fold body and head piece in half and join around most of curved edge. Fill with stuffing and sew closed.

WINGS

Make two, using chestnut brown

Cast on 5sts. Working in moss stitch throughout, **row 1:** k1, p1, k1, p1, k1. **Row 2:** p2 tog, k1, p1, inc one st into last st. **Row 3:** inc one st into first 2sts, p1, k2 tog. **Row 4:** *k1, p1, rep from * to end of row. **Row 5:** #p1, k1, rep from # to end of row. Rep last two rows. Cast off. Hide ends of yarn by sewing them back through knitting.

Sew cast-off edge of wing to chicken's body (see picture on p48 as guide).

BEAK

Make a 2.5cm (1in) single chain in mid brown (see Basic Techniques, p10). Hide ends of yarn by sewing them back along chain. Sew centre of chain to front of chicken's face, then bend in half in shape of beak and make stitches at beak's base to hold it in shape.

CRESTS

In red yarn, make one 5cm (2in) and one 2.5cm (1in) single

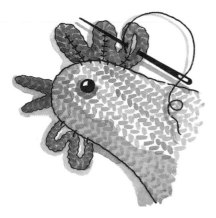

chain (see Basic Techniques, p10). Sew longer chain to head of chicken in three loops as crest (see diagram below left). Sew shorter chain in two loops under chicken's beak. Sew loops closed with extra stitches.

FEET

Push pipe-cleaner through chicken, from one side to the other. Bend ends of pipe-cleaner down to give two long dangling legs. Bend ends into three toes for each foot (see diagram below).

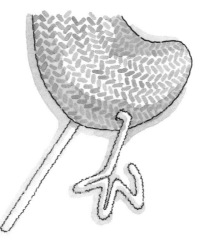

EYES

Sew one black bead on each side of head.

COCKEREL

To make a cockerel, follow instructions for chicken, then add tail as follows: make eight 7.5cm (3in) single chains in DK yarn – four in red and four in green (see Basic Techniques, p10). Hide ends of yarn by sewing them back along chains. Sew end of each chain to back of chicken, forming a clump.

CHICK

BODY AND HEAD

Make one, using yellow

The pieces of the chick are worked in smooth stocking stitch.

Cast on 6sts. P 1 row. Working in st-st throughout, inc one st at both ends of next and every foll k row until you have 12sts total.

Work 3 rows; [9 rows total]. K2 tog at both ends of next and every foll k row until 6sts rem. Work 3 rows; [17 rows total]. Cast off. This is the head end.

Fold body and head piece in half and join around most of curved edge. Fill with stuffing and sew closed.

WINGS

Make two, using yellow

Cast on 4sts. Working in st-st throughout and beg with a k row, work 4 rows.

Next row: k2 tog, k2 tog. **Next k row:** k2 tog. Break off yarn, slip end through rem st and pull tight. Hide end of yarn by sewing it back through knitting.

With smooth side upwards, sew cast on edge of wing to side of chick.

BEAK

Work as for chicken.

FEET

Work as for chicken, but use a shorter length of pipe cleaner and make triangles for feet instead of separate toes.

EYES

Sew stitches in black yarn on each side of head.

THE DEEP BLUE SEA

PEARL FISHERMAN

Approximate size: 29in (11½in)

When a small piece of grit or sand gets inside a pearl oyster, the oyster lets out a substance in an attempt to clean itself. But if the grit stays, more and more of the substance is released until finally it hardens and becomes a lustrous pearl. This is the prize that pearl fishermen seek as they dive, without the aid of oxygen tanks or modern diving equipment, into the tropical waters. They take a knife with them to open up each shell in the hope of finding the splendid pearl to sell to jewellers from rich countries. And best of all, if they find pearls of a similar colour or size, that can be matched up to become a necklace, then they may get extra money for their precious haul.

How easy is it to make?

Straightforward. The pieces aren't complicated. If you don't want to embroider the sarong, you could use a variegated wool instead to give the effect of a batik-dyed cloth. If you're making this toy for a small child, you may want to sew the costume in place on the pearl fisherman's body, to avoid pieces getting lost.

Needles: 3¼mm (size 10, US 3)

Yarn: 50g DK in skin colour; 20g DK in black; 20g DK in yellow; scraps of DK in dark brown, purple, red and pink

Pair 10mm (³/₈in) toy safety eyes

Tapestry and sewing needles

Dark brown thread

Two shell-shaped beads or buttons

Washable polyester toy stuffing

Props: thick card; glue; brown and silver paint for knife; a scrap of loose-weave fabric such as hessian for a fishing sack; extra shell-shaped beads to fill sack

Tension

Over st-st, using 3¼mm (size 10, US 3) needles, 26sts and 34 rows to 10cm (4in).

Also . . .

Figures in [square brackets] give the total number of stitches or rows you should have at that stage.

The Basic Person Pattern is on p12.

All the information you need to work the Pearl Fisherman is in Basic Techniques, p9–13.

BODY AND HEAD, ARMS, LEGS AND EARS

Work and make up as for Basic Person Pattern, using skin colour.

HAIR

Work as for Basic Person Pattern, using black.

MOUTH

Work as for Basic Person Pattern, using dark brown.

SARONG

Make one, using yellow

Cast on 70sts. Working in st-st throughout and beg with a k row, work 6 rows.

K2 tog at both ends of next and every foll k row until 54sts

rem. K or p2 tog at both ends of next and every foll row until 40sts rem. Cast off.

Press sarong piece with a warm iron. Sew a line of running stitch (see Basic Techniques, p11) around edge of sarong with yellow yarn. Pull gently to straighten and strengthen edge, then make a few stitches to secure yarn.

In coloured yarns, embroider big lazy daisies (see Basic Techniques, p11) all over the sarong.

Make a 40cm (16in) length of single chain in dark brown yarn. Sew a shell-shaped bead or button to each end. Use chain to tie sarong around fisherman's waist.

FINISHING TOUCHES

Knife: Trace knife pattern on to paper, cut it out and draw round it on to thick card. Cut out card shape. Paint blade silver and handle brown.

Bag: From a piece of loose-weave fabric, cut a circle about 15cm (6in) across. Sew a line of running stitch around edge and gather it up, leaving long ends of thread. Fill bag with shell-shaped beads or buttons.

Template for knife

DOLPHIN

Approximate size: 14cm (5½in)

Dolphins often display a real sense of fun – they love tumbling and leaping in the waves, and will happily join in with games and solve puzzles set for them by humans, especially if rewarded with a fish! People become very fond of them for these antics, but there is also a deeper relationship between dolphins and humans.

Individual dolphins will sometimes become fascinated by humans, and regularly visit a particular beach or fishing vessel. There are also many ancient legends of dolphins helping shipwrecked sailors, lifting an exhausted swimmer on to their back and carrying them to shore. The dolphin's intelligence, general friendliness and lack of aggression make them a favourite with everyone.

How easy is it to make?

Easy! This is a great toy for beginners to make – four simple pieces in a single colour. If you're a quick knitter, or once you've had some practice, you could easily make a whole school of dolphins in an evening!

Needles: 3mm (size 11, US 2)
Yarn: 25g DK in grey; scraps of DK in dark grey
Two black beads
Tapestry and sewing needles
Black thread
Washable polyester toy stuffing

Tension

Over st-st, using 3mm (size 11, US 2) needles, 28sts and 36 rows to 10cm (4in).

Also . . .

Figures in [square brackets] give the total number of stitches or rows you should have at that stage.

All the information you need to work the Dolphin is in Basic Techniques, p9–13.

BODY AND HEAD
Make one, using grey

Cast on 9sts. Working in st-st throughout and beg with a k row, work 2 rows.

Next row: inc one st into first st, k(2), inc one st into next st, k1, inc one st into next st, k to last st, inc one st into last st. **Next row:** p. Rep last 2 rows, with number of sts in brackets two more each time, until you have 29sts total. Work 5 rows; [16 rows total].

Next row: k7, turn and cast on 9sts (back of fin), turn and k to end of row; [38sts].

Next k row: k9, k2 tog, k1, k2 tog, k to end of row; [36sts]. **Next k row:** k8, k2 tog, k1, k2 tog, k to end of row; [34sts]. **Next k row:** k7, k2 tog, k1, k2 tog, k to end of row; [32sts]. **Next k row:** k6, k2 tog, k1, k2 tog, k to end of row; [30sts]. Work 11 rows; [36 rows total].

Next row: k2 tog, k(11), k2 tog, k2 tog, k to last 2sts, k2 tog. **Next row:** p. Rep last 2 rows, with number of sts in brackets 2 less each time, until 10sts rem. **Next row:** p. Cast off. This is the beak end.

With smooth sides together, fold body and head piece in half (inside out) and sew open edge of fin closed. Turn smooth sides out and fold body and head piece in half. Starting at beak end, join long side seam, fill with stuffing and sew closed.

Shaping the beak: about 2.5cm (1in) from front of dolphin, sew a line of stitching in matching yarn to pinch end of beak (see picture below as guide).

FLIPPERS
Make two, using grey

Cast on 6sts. Working in st-st throughout and beg with a k row, work 2 rows.

Next row: inc one st into first st, k1, inc one st into next 2sts, k1, inc one st into last st; [10sts]. Work 3 rows.

Next k row: (k2 tog, k1, k2 tog) twice; [6sts]. Next k row: k2 tog three times; [3sts]. **Next k row:** k3 tog. Break off yarn, slip end through rem st and pull tight.

With smooth sides outwards, fold flipper piece in half and join around edge. Ladderstitch to body, catching side of flipper with a few stitches to make it lie flat along side of body.

TAIL
Make one, using grey

Cast on 8sts. Working in st-st throughout and beg with a k row, work 2 rows.

Next row: inc one st into first st, k2, inc one st into next 2sts, k2, inc one st into last st; [12sts]. **Next k row:** inc one st into first st, k4, inc one st into next 2sts, k4, inc one st into last st; [16sts]. **Next k row:** inc one st into first st, k6, inc one st into next 2sts, k6, inc one st into last st; [20sts]. Work 3 rows. Cast off.

The tail piece is shaped like a diamond. With smooth sides outwards, fold it in half so that the two narrower points meet. Join around two edges, fill with stuffing then sew closed. Ladderstitch to end of body.

Finishing the dolphin

EYE PATCHES

With dark grey yarn, embroider two stitches on each side of head, using Swiss darning (see Basic Techniques, p11). With black thread, sew a black bead on top of each eye patch.

MOUTH

With black yarn, sew two large stitches outwards from point of beak, for a mouth.

SHARK

Approximate size: 28cm (11in)

Sharks get a very bad press – they have the reputation for attacking people indiscriminately and lurking just off tropical beaches to ambush unwary swimmers. But in fact only a few species of shark are large enough even to think of taking on a meal as big as a human being! Nevertheless, they have found themselves a place in human stories as sinister killers, with a dark, brooding personality. Cutting through the water, their characteristic dorsal fin strikes fear into the heart of many a fisherman or diver. But what appears to be restless energy (the shark swimming backwards and forwards off the shore or around a boat), which some think shows the shark's malevolence, may well be put down to the fact that sharks have to keep swimming to stay alive. Unlike dolphins and whales, which take breaths of air just as we do, the shark needs to have water constantly passing by its breathing gills in order to absorb essential oxygen from the ocean.

How easy is it to make?

Easy! All worked in a single colour, the pieces are simple to make.

> *Needles: 3¼mm (size 10, US 3)*
>
> *Yarn: 20g DK in grey; scraps of DK in black*
>
> *Two black beads*
>
> *Tapestry and sewing needles*
>
> *Black thread*
>
> *Washable polyester toy stuffing*

Tension

Over st-st, using 3¼mm (size 10, US 3) needles, 26sts and 34 rows to 10cm (4in).

Also . . .

Figures in [square brackets] give the total number of stitches or rows you should have at that stage.

All the information you need to work the Shark is in Basic Techniques, p9–13.

BODY AND HEAD
Make one, using grey

Cast on 10sts. Working in st-st throughout and beg with a k row, work 2 rows.

Next row: inc one st into first st, k(3), inc one st into next 2sts, k to last st, inc one st into last st. Work 3 rows. Rep last 4 rows, with number of sts in brackets 2 more each time, until you have 34sts total. Work 11 rows; [34 rows total].

Next row: k17, turn and cast on 12sts (back of fin), turn and k to end of row; [46sts]. Work 3 rows.

Next row: k(21), k2 tog, k2 tog, k to end of row. **Next row:** p. Rep last 2 rows, with number of sts in brackets 1 less each time, until 32sts rem.

Next k row: (k2 tog, k12, k2 tog) twice; [28sts]. Work 5 rows; [58 rows total]. **Next row:** (k2 tog, k10, k2 tog) twice; [24sts]. Work 5 rows; [64 rows total]. **Next row:** (k2 tog, k8, k2 tog) twice; [20sts]. Work 5 rows; [70 rows total].

Next row: (k2 tog, k2 tog, k4) twice, k2 tog, k2 tog; [14sts]. **Next k row:** k2 tog, k2 tog, k6, k2 tog, k2 tog; [10sts]. Work 5 rows; [78 rows total]. **Next row:** (k2 tog, k1, k2 tog) twice; [6sts]. **Next row:** p. Cast off. This is the nose end.

With smooth sides together, fold body and head piece in half (inside out) and sew open edge of fin closed. Turn smooth sides out and fold body and head piece in half. Starting at nose end, join long seam, fill with stuffing then sew closed.

TAIL
Make one, using grey

Cast on 2sts. Working in st-st throughout and beg with a k row, work 2 rows.

Next row: inc one st into both sts; [4sts]. **Next k row:** inc one st into each st; [8sts]. **Next k row:** inc one st into first st, k2, inc one st into next 2sts, k2, inc one st into last st; [12sts]. Work 29 rows; [36 rows total].

Next row: (k2 tog, k2, k2 tog) twice; [8sts]. **Next k row:** k2 tog four times; [4sts]. **Next k row:** k2 tog, k2 tog; [2sts]. **Next row:** p. Cast off.

With smooth sides outwards, fold tail piece in half. Join along side seam, filling with stuffing as you go. Sew closed.

About 7.5cm (3in) from one end, attach a length of matching yarn to the tail with a few sts. Wind yarn around tail and pull tight. Secure yarn with a few sts, then use end of yarn to sew tail to end of body. Pinch tail into a shallow V shape (see picture on p67 as guide). Hold in shape with a few stitches in the inside angle of the V.

SIDE FINS
Make two, using grey

Cast on 6sts. Working in st-st throughout and beg with a k row, work 2 rows.

Next row: inc one st into first st, k1, inc one st into next 2sts, k1, inc one st into last st; [10sts]. Work 5 rows; [8 rows total].

Next row: (k2 tog, k1, k2 tog) twice; [6sts]. **Next k row:** k2 tog three times; [3sts]. **Next k row:** k3 tog. Break off yarn, slip end through rem st and pull tight.

With smooth sides outwards, fold fin piece in half and join around edge. Ladderstitch to body, catching side of fin with a few stitches to make it lie flat along side of body.

SMALL REAR FINS
Make two, using grey

Cast on 8sts. Working in st-st throughout and beg with a k row, work 2 rows.

K2 tog at both ends of next and every foll k row until 2sts rem. **Next k row:** k2 tog. Break off yarn, slip end through rem st and pull tight.

With smooth sides outwards, fold fin piece in half and join around edge. Ladderstitch to body – one on top of tail, halfway between main fin and tail; the other on the bottom of the body, nearer the tail (see picture on p67 as guide).

EYES

With black thread, sew a black bead to each side of head.

MOUTH

With black yarn, sew two large stitches outwards from under the pointed nose (see picture on p67 as guide).

KILLER WHALE

Approximate size: 14.5cm (5³/₄in)

Although they have a daunting array of teeth, and despite their name, killer whales aren't dangerous to humans. But they are very effective hunters. Like wolves of the sea, they travel in hunting packs, so their prey stand little chance of getting away. The killer whales communicate with a series of squeals and clicks that travel through the water in waves, like sound in air, allowing their companions to work out where to position themselves to block the escape of an unwary shoal of salmon, or a seal stranded from its own protective group.

How easy is it to make?

Challenging. The pieces are easy and quick to knit. Only the markings, worked as embroidery, take a little extra time. If you're making this toy for a small child, substitute the bead eyes with stitched eyes worked in blue or green yarn.

Needles: Size 11 (3mm, US 2)

Yarn: 25g DK in black; scraps of DK in white and grey

Two black beads

Tapestry and sewing needles

Black thread

Washable polyester toy stuffing

Tension

Over st-st, using size 11 (3mm, US 2) needles, 28sts and 36 rows to 10cm (4in).

Also . . .

Figures in [square brackets] give the total number of stitches or rows you should have at that stage.

All the information you need to work the Killer Whale is in Basic Techniques, p9–13.

BODY AND HEAD
Make one, using black
Work and make up as for dolphin body and head, p66.

FLIPPER
Make two, using black
Work and make up as for dolphin flipper, p66, and ladderstitch to side of body, making extra stitches to make flipper lie along side of killer whale's body.

TAIL
Make one, using black
Work and make up as for dolphin tail, p66, and ladderstitch to end of body.

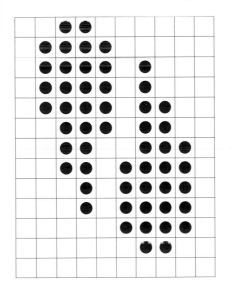

Finishing the killer whale

PATCHES
With white yarn, embroider patches of white markings on the killer whale, using Swiss darning (see Basic Techniques, p11, picture on p63 and chart as guides). Make lower half of killer whale completely white, tapering out to black towards tail.

Eye patches: With white yarn, embroider a patch on either side of the killer whale's head, using Swiss darning and following the chart. With black thread, sew a black bead at front point of each eye patch.

MOUTH
With grey yarn, sew two large stitches outwards from point of beak.

Swiss darning chart for killer whale eye patches

TURTLE

Approximate size: 25cm (10in)

Just as you can tell the age of a tree by counting the rings in its trunk, so can you tell the age of a turtle by counting the rings on its shell. In this turtle toy, the rings are represented by patterns worked in combinations of plain and purl stitch. As turtles grow, more rings appear, showing that some turtles can live for many decades. And the life they lead is very hard, so there are also other signs of the turtle's experience marked on the shell. There might be barnacles and small clumps of seaweed, making the turtle's shell their home. But there might also be great scars and gouges, caused by attacks from sharks and fishermen. Turtles are considered a great delicacy in many parts of the world, and they have been hunted so much that there are now very few left.

But increasingly, the turtles are being protected. Special beaches are set aside so that the mother turtles can haul themselves out of the water to dig a sandy nest and lay their eggs inside. When the eggs hatch, the first test the baby turtles go through is to struggle down to the sea which will become their home. If they succeed, they stand a chance of growing up to be a magnificent turtle, swimming gracefully through the ocean.

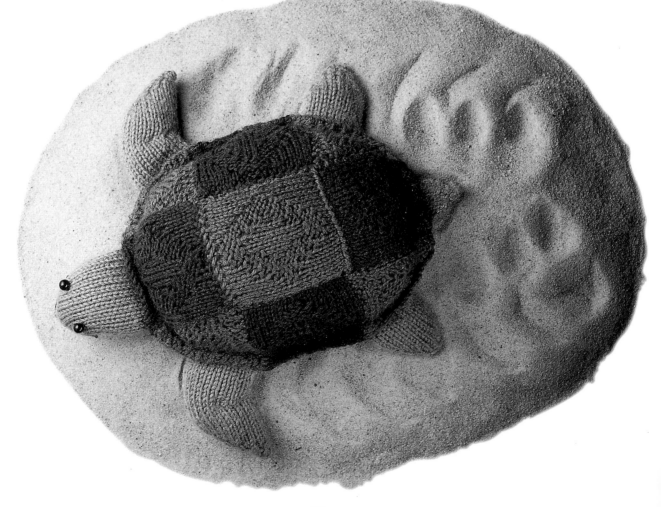

How easy is it to make?

Straightforward. There are quite a few pieces for this toy. But work through them methodically, and you should find it quite easy to make. If you don't feel confident enough to work the plain and purl pattern to give your turtle ring patterns on its shell, instructions for a simpler plain shell are included after each shell section.

Needles: 3mm (size 11, US 2)

Yarn: 50g DK in dusty green; 20g DK in dark green; 20g DK in mid green; scraps of DK in black

Two black beads

Tapestry and sewing needles

Black thread

Washable polyester toy stuffing

Tension

Over st-st, using 3mm (size 11, US 2) needles, 28sts and 36 rows to 10cm (4in).

Also . . .

Figures in [square brackets] give the total number of stitches or rows you should have at that stage.

All the information you need to work the Turtle is in Basic Techniques, p9–13.

SHELL SQUARE
Make four, using dark green; one, using mid green
Cast on 16sts. **Row 1:** k. **Row 2:** p7, k2, p7. **Row 3:** k6, p4, k6. **Row 4:** p6, k4, p6. **Row 5:** k5, p6, k5. **Row 6:** p5, k2, p2, k2, p5. **Row 7:** k4, p3, k2, p3, k4. **Row 8:** p4, k3, p2, k3, p4. **Row 9:** k3, p3, k4, p3, k3. **Row 10:** p3, k3, p4, k3, p3. **Row 11:** k2, p3, k6, p3, k2. **Row 12:** p2, k3, p6, k3, p2. **Row 13:** rep row 9. **Row 14:** rep row 10. **Row 15:** rep row 7. **Row 16:** rep row 8. **Row 17:** rep row 5. **Row 18:** rep

row 6. **Row 19:** rep row 3. **Row 20:** rep row 4. **Row 21:** k7, p2, k7. **Row 22:** p. Cast off.
Alternatively, for simple plain shell squares: Cast on 16sts. Beg with a k row, st-st 22 rows. Cast off.

SHELL TRIANGLES
Make four, using mid green
Cast on 20sts. **Row 1:** k. **Row 2:** p. **Row 3:** k2 tog, k2, p12, k2, k2 tog; [18sts]. **Row 4:** p3, k12, p3. **Row 5:** k2 tog, k2, p3, k4, p3, k2, k2 tog; [16sts]. **Row 6:** p3, k3, p4, k3, p3. **Row 7:** k2 tog, k2, p3, k2, p3, k2, k2 tog; [14sts]. **Row 8:** p3, k3, p2, k3, p3. **Row 9:** k2 tog, k2, p6, k2, k2 tog; [12sts]. **Row 10:** p3, k6, p3. **Row 11:** k2 tog, k2, p4, k2, k2 tog; [10sts]. **Row 12:** p3, k4, p3. **Row 13:** k2 tog, k2, p2, k2, k2 tog; [8sts]. **Row 14:** p3, k2, p3. **Row 15:** k2 tog, k4, k2 tog; [6sts]. **Row 16:** p. **Row 17:** k2 tog, k2, k2 tog; [4sts]. **Row 18:** p. **Row 19:** k2 tog, k2 tog; [2sts]. **Row 20:** p2 tog.
Break off yarn, slip end through rem st and pull tight.
Alternatively, for simple plain shell triangles: Cast on 20sts. Working in st-st throughout and beg with a k row, work 2 rows. K2 tog at both ends of next and every foll k row until 4sts rem. **Next row:** k2 tog, k2 tog; [2sts]. **Next row:** p2 tog. Break off yarn, slip end through rem st and pull tight.

BACK FOOT
Make two, using dusty green
Cast on 20sts. Working in st-st throughout and beg with a k row, work 10 rows.
Next row: (k2 tog, k6, k2 tog) twice; [16sts]. **Next k row:** (k2 tog, k4, k2 tog) twice; [12sts]. **Next k row:** (k2 tog, k2, k2 tog) twice; [8sts]. **Next

k row:** k2 tog four times; [4sts]. **Next k row:** k2 tog, k2 tog; [2sts]. **Next k row:** k2 tog. Break off yarn, slip end through rem st and pull tight.
With smooth sides outwards, fold foot piece in half. Join side seam, fill with stuffing then sew closed.

FRONT FLIPPER
Make two, using dusty green
Cast on 20sts. Working in st-st throughout and beg with a k row, work 22 rows. Foll pattern for back foot from * to end.
With smooth sides outwards, fold flipper piece in half. Join side, fill with stuffing then sew closed. About 5cm (2in) from pointed end, bend flipper at a slight angle and ladderstitch in position (see picture opposite as guide).

TAIL
Make two, using dusty green
Cast on 8sts. Working in st-st throughout and beg with a k row, work 6 rows.
K2 tog at both ends of next and every foll k row until 2sts rem. **Next row:** p **Next row:** k2 tog. Break off yarn, slip end through rem st and pull tight.
With smooth sides outwards, match up 2 tail pieces and join around edge.

UNDERBELLY
Make one, using dusty green
Cast on 14sts. Working in st-st throughout and beg with a k row, work 2 rows.
Inc one st at both ends of next and every foll k row, until you have 34sts total. Work 23 rows; [44 rows total]. K2 tog at both ends of next and every foll k row until 14sts rem. **Next row:** p. Cast off.

HEAD
Make one, using dusty green
Cast on 28sts. Working in st-st throughout and beg with a k row, work 18 rows.

Next row: (k5, k2 tog, k2 tog, k5) twice; [24sts]. **Next row:** (p4, p2 tog, p2 tog, p4) twice; [20sts]. **Next row:** (k3, k2 tog, k2 tog, k3) twice; [16sts]. **Next row:** (p2, p2 tog, p2 tog, p2) twice; [12sts]. **Next row:** (k1, k2 tog, k2 tog, k1) twice; [8sts]. **Next row:** p2 tog four times; [4sts]. **Next row:** k2 tog, k2 tog; [2sts]. **Next row:** p2 tog. Break off yarn, slip end through rem st and pull tight.

With smooth sides outwards, fold head piece in half. Join along straight edge. This seam runs down the middle of the underside of the head. Fill with stuffing then sew closed. About 5cm (2in) from pointed end, bend head down at a slight angle and ladderstitch in position (see picture on p63 as guide).

MAKING UP THE SHELL

Lay mid green central shell square on a flat surface. Arrange other four squares around it to form a cross and place triangles in corners of cross (see below). Piece by piece, join squares and triangles together, forming a slightly domed shell shape (see picture on p70 as guide).

Work a line of running stitch close to the edge of the shell, and pull the yarn gently without gathering the edge. This will help to neaten edge of shell.

VARIATIONS

This pattern could also be knitted up as a slow-moving, woolly-footed tortoise. Simply substitute mid brown for four of the shell squares; dark brown for shell triangles and central shell square; and light brown for head, feet and underbelly. Instead of making front flippers, make four legs the same following the turtle's back leg pattern.

The turtle can also be made as a hand puppet. Knit a second underbelly piece, and make up the turtle as follows. Join and stuff the shell and first underbelly as for the ordinary turtle, and attach the tail.

ATTACHING UNDERBELLY

Hold shell upside down and fill with stuffing. Place underbelly over opening and sew it in place around edge, about 1cm (1/2 in) in from shell's edge, leaving a slight lip.

ATTACHING HEAD, TAIL, FEET AND FLIPPERS

Ladderstitch head, tail, feet and flippers to underbelly, close to edge of shell.

EYES

With black thread, sew two black beads to face (see photograph on p70 as guide).

When making the limbs and head, don't stuff them or close off the ends. Sew only the top half of each piece to the underside of the turtle.

With the turtle upside down, place the second underbelly on top of the first underbelly. Sew it to the bottom sections of each limb and the head, and join it to the first underbelly in between the limbs and between the head and the flippers. Leave enough of the second underbelly open at the back of the turtle to allow a hand to slip inside. You may want to stuff the head slightly to keep it in shape.

MOUTH

With black yarn, make two big stitches outwards from point of turtle's face.

OCTOPUS

Approximate size: Body 25cm (10in); Tentacles 46cm (18in)

An octopus will never venture on to land, because it would become floppy and cumbersome, unable to lift its legs off the ground. In the water, in comparison, its natural buoyancy means that its limbs move like the arms of a dancer – graceful waving tentacles that help the octopus move across the ocean floor, seeking food. These limbs also give the octopus its name, which means, quite simply, 'eight feet'. Only when startled does the octopus become more animated, darting quickly into a rocky hiding place, and squirting a black ink-like substance into the water behind it to confuse its attacker.

How easy is it to make?

Easy! There are only three pattern pieces (although you'll have to make eight legs!), all worked in the same colour.

> *Needles: 4mm (size 8, US 5)*
>
> *Yarn: 150g DK in blue; scraps of DK in black*
>
> *Scraps of black, blue and white felt*
>
> *Tapestry and sewing needles*
>
> *Thread in black, blue and white*
>
> *Washable polyester toy stuffing*

Tension

Over st-st, using 4mm (size 8, US 5) needles, 20sts and 28 rows to 10cm (4in).

Also . . .

Figures in [square brackets] give the total number of stitches or rows you should have at that stage.

All the information you need to work the Octopus is in Basic Techniques, p9–13.

HEAD

Make one, using blue
Cast on 90sts. Working in st-st throughout and beg with a k row, work 6 rows.

Next row: inc one st into first st, k42, k2 tog, k2 tog, k to last st, inc one st into last st; [90sts]. **Next row:** p. Rep last 2 rows twice more; [12 rows total].Work 32 rows; [44 rows total].

Next row: k(43), k2 tog, k2 tog, k to end of row. **Next row:** p. Rep last 2 rows, with number of sts in brackets 1 less each time, until 74sts rem.

Next k row: *(k2 tog, k3) seven times, k2 tog, rep from * to end of row; [58sts]. **Next k row:** k2 tog, k1, (k2 tog, k2) six times, k2 tog, k2 tog, (k2 tog, k2) six times, k1, k2 tog; [42sts]. **Next k row:** (k1, k2 tog) seven times, (k2 tog, k1) seven times; [28sts]. **Next row:** p. Cast off. This is the top edge of the head.

With smooth sides outwards, fold head piece in half. Join top and side seams and fill with stuffing.

BASE

Make one, using blue
Cast on 14sts. Working in st-st throughout and beg with a k row, work 2 rows.

Next row: inc one st into first 2sts, k to last 2sts, inc one st into last 2sts. **Next row:** p. Rep last 2 rows until you have 42sts total. Work 37 rows; [52 rows total].

Next row: k2 tog, k2 tog, k to last 4sts, k2 tog, k2 tog. **Next row:** p. Rep last 2 rows until 14sts rem. **Next row:** p. Cast off.

With smooth side outwards, place base piece over open end of head and sew in position.

LEGS

Make eight, using blue
Cast on 20sts. Working in st-st throughout and beg with a k row, work 80 rows.

Next row: (k2 tog, k6, k2 tog) twice; [16sts]. **Next k row:** (k2 tog, k4, k2 tog) twice; [12sts]. **Next k row:** (k2 tog, k2, k2 tog) twice; [8sts]. **Next row:** p. Cast off.

With smooth sides outwards, fold leg piece in half lengthways. Join shaped end and long side seam, then fill with stuffing.

Once all the legs are made, position them around the body (see the diagram below). Sew open ends of legs to bottom edge of head.

EYES

Trace eye pattern pieces on to paper and cut them out. Draw round circles on felt and cut them out: cut two pupils in black; two middle-sized circles in blue and two large circles in white.

Sew blue circle to white circle, and black pupil on top of blue circle (see picture on p73 as guide). Sew eye to octopus's head.

MOUTH

With black yarn, sew a small V-shaped mouth (see picture on p73 as guide).

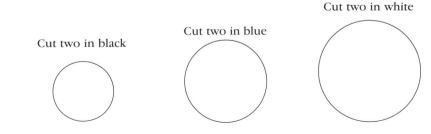

Cut two in black

Cut two in blue

Cut two in white

Templates for felt eyes of octopus

CLOWNFISH

Approximate size: 25cm (10in)

The clownfish has bold white stripes bordered by black bands, like the striking make-up of circus clowns. They dart about in the maze-like reefs of the South Pacific, a flash of colour amid the fronds of seaweed and giant sea anemones. The clownfish has a close relationship with the sea anemone, dependent on its stinging 'tentacles' as a safe place to live. It will attack marauding tropical fish and even bring plankton food to the anemone to repay its debt.

How easy is it to make?

Straightforward. The fins are knitted in rib stitch, and there's quite a bit of colour changing. But there are only three types of pieces to make, so it shouldn't be too challenging.

Needles: 3mm (Size 11, US2)

Yarn: 20g DK in orange; 10g DK in white; a small amount (less than 10g) DK in black

Tapestry needle

Washable polyester toy stuffing

Tension

Over st-st, using 3mm (Size 11, US2) needles, 28sts and 36 rows to 10cm (4in).

Also...

Figures in [square brackets] give the total number of stitches or rows you should have at that stage.

All the information you need to work the Clownfish is in Basic Techniques, p9–13.

BODY AND HEAD
Make one, using orange, black and white
Cast on 32sts in orange.
Working in st-st throughout and beg with a k row, work 6 rows. Change to black. Work 2 rows. Change to white. Work 8 rows. Change to

black. Work 2 rows. Change to orange.
Next row: inc one st into first st, k(14), inc one st into next 2sts, k to last st, inc one st into last st. **Next row:** p. Rep last 2 rows, with number of sts in brackets 2 more each time, until you have 56sts total. **Next row:** p.
*Change to black (see Basic Techniques, p10, for how to join a new colour). Work 2 rows. Change to white. Work 8 rows. Change to black. Work 2 rows.** Change to orange. Work 12 rows. Rep once from * to **. Change to orange. Work 2 rows.
Next row: k2 tog, k2 tog, (k20), k2 tog four times, k to last 4sts, k2 tog, k2 tog. **Next row:** p. Rep last 2 rows, with number of sts in brackets 4 less each time, until 16sts rem.
Next k row: k2 tog eight times. **Next row:** p. Break off yarn, slip end through rem sts and pull tight.
With smooth sides outwards, fold body and head piece in half. Join around edge, leaving an opening. Fill with stuffing, then sew closed.

TAIL AND SIDE FINS
Make three, using black and orange
Cast on 37sts in black. **Row 1:** (p2, k5) five times, p2. **Row 2:** (k2, p5) five times, k2.
Change to orange, rep rows 1 and 2 twice.

Row 7: (p2, k2 tog, k1, k2 tog) five times, p2. **Row 8:** (k2, p3) five times, k2. **Row 9:** (p2, k3 tog) five times, p2. **Row 10:** (k2, p1) five times, k2. **Row 11:** (p2, k1) five times, p2. Cast off.
Hide ends of yarn by sewing them back through knitting. Sew cast-off edge of one piece to narrow end of body. Sew cast-off edges of remaining pieces to side of fish (see picture on p72).

TOP AND BOTTOM FINS
Make three, using black and orange
Cast on 23sts in black. **Row 1:** (p2, k5) three times, p2. **Row 2:** (k2, p5) three times, k2.
Change to orange, rep rows 1 and 2.
Row 5: (p2, k2 tog, k1, k2 tog) three times, p2. **Row 6:** (k2, p3) three times, k2. **Row 7:** (p2, k3 tog) three times, p2. **Row 8:** (k2, p1) three times, k2. Cast off.
Hide ends of yarn by sewing them back through knitting. Forming fin pieces into half-circle shapes, sew cast-off edge of one piece to bottom of fish, and of remaining two pieces to top of fish (see picture on p72 as guide).

FACE
With black yarn, sew a line for a mouth and two big spots for eyes (see picture on p72 as guide).

FOREST FRIENDS

CANADIAN MOUNTIE

Approximate size: 29cm (11½in)

Mounties, in their splendid red uniforms, always cut a dashing figure as they uphold the law in Canada. Their costume still reflects their history, with brown jodhpur-style trousers suitable for riding the horses which gave the Mounties their name – 'Mounted policemen'. But these days, horses are only used for specific jobs and special occasions. Mounties are much more likely to be seen travelling around the beautiful Canadian landscape in a police car. They patrol some of the most spectacular places on earth.

How easy is it to make?

Straightforward. The pieces aren't complicated. The hat and jacket may take a little extra time to complete. If you're making this toy for a small child, you may want to sew the costume in place on the Mountie's body, to avoid pieces getting lost.

Needles: 3 ¼mm (size 10, US 3)

Yarn: 50g DK in skin colour; 40g DK in red and mid brown; 40g DK in dark brown; 10g DK in black

Pair 10mm (³/8 in) toy safety eyes

Tapestry and sewing needles

Dark brown thread

Washable polyester toy stuffing

Tension

Over st-st, using 3¼mm (size 10, US 3) needles, 26sts and 34 rows to 10cm (4in).

Also . . .

Figures in [square brackets] give the total number of stitches or rows you should have at that stage.

The Basic Person Pattern is on p12.

All the information you need to work the Canadian Mountie is in Basic Techniques, p9–13.

BODY AND HEAD
Make one, using mid brown, black and skin colour
Work as for Basic Person Pattern, using following colours: first 12 rows in mid brown; next 3 rows in black; rem rows in skin colour. Make up as for Basic Person Pattern.

LEGS
Make two, using dark brown and mid brown
Work as for Basic Person Pattern

using following colours: work first 22 rows in dark brown; rem rows in mid brown.
Make up as for Basic Person Pattern and ladderstitch to body.

ARMS AND EARS
Make two of each, using skin colour
Work and make up as for Basic Person Pattern, and ladderstitch to body.

MOUTH
Work as for Basic Person Pattern, using dark brown.

HAIR
Work as for Basic Person Pattern, using black.

JACKET SLEEVES
Make two, using red
Cast on 26sts. Working in st-st throughout and beg with a k row, work 26 rows.
K2 tog at both ends and once

near middle of next and every foll k row until 11sts rem, ending with a k row. K 2 rows. Cast off.

With smooth sides outwards, fold sleeve piece in half and join side seam up to start of shaping. Roll end of sleeve up to form cuff and stitch in place.

JACKET RIGHT FRONT

Make one, using red

Cast on 14sts. K 2 rows. Working in st-st throughout and beg with a k row, work 22 rows; [24 rows total]. K2 tog at end of next and every foll k row until 8sts rem, ending with a k row. K 2 rows. Cast off.

JACKET LEFT FRONT

Make one, using red

Cast on 14sts. K 2 rows. Cont in st-st, and beg with a k row, work 8 rows.

The next 2 rows will make the first buttonhole, near the edge of the jacket front.

First buttonhole row: *k to last 3sts. From left, imagine rem sts are numbered 1, 2 & 3. K sts 3 and 2, pass st 3 over st 2 (cast it off), then k st 1.

Second buttonhole row: p2, turn and cast on one st, turn and p to end of row. Work 8 rows; [20 rows total].

To make the second buttonhole, rep first and second buttonhole rows.

Work 2 rows. K2 tog at beg of next and every foll k row until 10sts rem.

To make the third buttonhole, next k row: k2 tog, rep from * to end of first buttonhole row. Rep second buttonhole row.

Next k row: k2 tog, k to end of row. K 2 rows. Cast off.

Sew around buttonholes with buttonhole stitch (see Basic Techniques, p10).

JACKET BACK

Make one, using red

Cast on 32sts. K 2 rows. Working in st-st throughout and beg with a k row, work 22 rows.

Next row: cast off 3sts, k to end of row; [29sts]. **Next row:** cast off 3sts, p to end of row; [26sts]. K2 tog at both ends of next and every foll k row until 14sts rem. K 2 rows. Cast off.

Lay jacket back with smooth side down. With smooth sides up, lay jacket left and right front pieces on top of jacket back, with long straight edges of front pieces overlapping in the centre. Join side seams up to start of shaping. Position sleeves on either side of jacket and join sleeves to armholes of jacket.

STRAP

Make one, using dark brown

Make an 80cm (32in) single chain in brown yarn (see Basic Techniques, p10). Fold length in half, and join two sections along their length to make a thick strap. Drape strap across Mountie's shoulder at a diagonal (see picture on p78 as guide). Take strap over to back of Mountie then around waist. Where strap meets, at front and behind, make a few stitches to hold it in place.

POUCH

Make one, using dark brown

Cast on 8sts. Working in st-st throughout and beg with a k row, work 30 rows.

K2 tog at both ends of next and every foll k row until 2sts rem. Break off yarn, slip end through rem sts and pull tight.

Fold pouch piece in three and join side seams. Sew pouch shut and stitch in position on belt (see picture on p78 as guide).

HAT BRIM

Make one, using dark brown

Cast on 108sts. K 2 rows. Working in st-st and beg with a k row, next row: (k2 tog, k14, k2 tog) six times; [96sts]. **Next k row:** (k2 tog, k12, k2 tog) six times; [84sts]. **Next k row:** (k2 tog, k10, k2 tog) six times; [72sts]. **Next k row:** (k2 tog, k8, k2 tog) six times; [60sts]. **Next row:** p. Cast off. Join short straight edges of brim to form full circle.

HAT TOP

Make one, using dark brown

Cast on 60sts. Working in st-st throughout and beg with a k row, work 4 rows.

Next row: (k2 tog, k6, k2 tog) six times; [48sts]. **Next k row:** (k2 tog, k4, k2 tog) six times; [36sts]. **Next k row:** (k2 tog, k2, k2 tog) six times; [24sts]. **Next k row:** k2 tog twelve times; [12sts]. **Next row:** p. Break off yarn, slip end through rem sts and pull tight.

With smooth sides outwards, fold hat piece in half. Join side seam to form dome. Sew base of dome to inner edge of brim. Work a line of running stitch (see Basic Techniques, p11) close to outer edge of brim in dark brown yarn. Pull yarn gently to strengthen and straighten edge. Secure end of yarn by making a few stitches.

HORSE

To make a horse for your Mountie, follow the zebra pattern on p96. Use dark grey yarn for the hooves (initial unstriped section of each leg), and light grey for all remaining pieces. Make a mane from lengths of yarn held in place by a line of stitches along the horse's neck (see picture on p79 as guide).

Use a scrap of brown felt for a saddle and single chain for a harness.

GRIZZLY BEAR

Approximate sizes: Adult 38cm (15in); Baby 25cm (10in)

Grizzly bears are solitary hunters, trekking through the woods and forests of North America and Canada for mile upon mile, often not seeing another bear for many weeks. Only in salmon season do they venture in great numbers down to the river. Dozens of bears are then seen wading through the icy water to take advantage of a great feast on offer there – thousands of salmon making their way upstream to breed. With a skilful flick of the paw, a mother bear will send a glistening salmon flying through the air to her cub waiting on the bank, who has been too nervous to plunge in the river and join in with the fishing.

How easy is it to make?

Challenging. The pieces aren't complicated, but the adult bear is quite a big project – a real armful for a small child! If you haven't got much time, try knitting the cub, which is rated as straightforward, instead.

For both bears

Needles: 3 1/4mm (size 10, US 3)

Tapestry and sewing needles

Black thread

Washable polyester toy stuffing

For the adult bear

Yarn: 100g DK in dark brown; scraps of DK in black

Pair 14mm (1/2 in) toy safety eyes

For the baby bear

Yarn: 60g DK in dark brown; scraps of DK in black

Pair 10mm (3/8in) toy safety eyes

Tension

Over st-st, using 3 1/4mm (size 10, US 3) needles, 26sts and 34 rows to 10cm (4in).

Also . . .

Figures in [square brackets] give the total number of stitches or rows you should have at that stage.

All the information you need to work the Grizzly Bears is in Basic Techniques, p9–13.

ADULT BEAR

BODY AND HEAD
Make one, using dark brown

Cast on 24sts. P 1 row. Working in st-st throughout, next row: inc one st into first 2sts, k(8), inc one st into next 4sts, k to last 2sts, inc one st into last 2sts. **Next row:** p. Rep last 2 rows, with number of sts in brackets 4 more each time, until you have 72sts total.

Next k row: inc one st into first st, k34, inc one st into next 2sts, k34, inc one st into last st; [76sts]. Work 23 rows; [37 rows total].

Next row: k2 tog, k(34), k2 tog, k2 tog, k to last 2sts, k2 tog. **Next row:** p. Rep last 2 rows, with number of sts in brackets 2 less each time, until 60sts rem. Work 7 rows; [51 rows total].

Next k row: k29, inc one st into next 2sts, k to end of row.

Next k row: k(29), inc one st into next 4sts, k to end of row. **Next row:** p. Rep last 2 rows, with number of sts in brackets 2 more each time, until you have 78sts total. Work 3 rows; [63 rows total].

K2 tog at both ends of next and every foll k row until 72sts rem.

Next k row: k2 tog, k(32), k2 tog, k2 tog, k to last 2sts, k2 tog. **Next row:** p. Rep last 2 rows, with number of sts in brackets 2 less each time, until 48sts rem.

Next k row: k(22), k2 tog, k2 tog, k to end of row. **Next row:** p. Rep last 2 rows, with number of sts in brackets 1 less each time, until 40sts rem.

Next k row: (k2 tog, k2 tog, k12, k2 tog, k2 tog) twice; [32sts]. Work 13 rows; [103 rows total].

Next row: k2 tog, k2 tog, k to last 4sts, k2 tog, k2 tog. **Next row:** p. Rep last 2 rows until 20sts rem. **Next row:** p. Cast off. This is the nose end.

With smooth sides outwards, fold body and head piece in half. Join nose and long seam (which runs down centre of underside of bear). Position and fit toy safety eyes. Fill with stuffing and sew closed.

LEGS
Make four, using dark brown
Cast on 14sts. This is the paw end. Working in st-st throughout and beg with a k row, work 2 rows.

Next row: inc one st into first st, k(5), inc one st into next 2sts, k to last st, inc one st into last st. **Next row:** p. Rep last 2 rows, with number of sts in brackets 2 more each time, until you have 30sts total. Work 41 rows; [50 rows total]. Cast off.

With smooth sides outwards, fold leg piece in half. Join paw end and side seam. Fill with stuffing and sew closed. Ladderstitch leg to body.

Paw: About 7.5cm (3in) up from end of leg, bend paw up at right angles to leg and ladderstitch in position.

EARS
Make two, using dark brown
Cast on 28sts. Working in st-st throughout and beg with a k row, work 10 rows. **Next row:** (k2 tog, k10, k2 tog) twice; [24sts]. **Next k row:** (k2 tog, k8, k2 tog) twice; [20sts]. **Next k row:** (k2 tog, k6, k2 tog) twice; [16sts]. **Next row:** p. Cast off.

With smooth sides outwards, fold ear piece in half. Join around edge and ladderstitch to head.

TAIL
Make one, using dark brown
Cast on 10sts. Working in st-st throughout and beg with a k row, work 6 rows.

Next row: (k2 tog, k1, k2 tog) twice; [6sts]. **Next k row:** k2 tog three times; [3sts]. **Next k row:** k3 tog. Break off yarn, slip end through rem st and pull tight. Hide end of yarn by sewing it back through knitting.

With smooth side outwards, sew tail piece to back of bear.

BEAR CUB

BODY AND HEAD
Make one, using dark brown
Cast on 16sts. P 1 row. Working in st-st throughout, next row: inc one st into first 2sts, k(4), inc one st into next 4sts, k to last 2sts, inc one st into last 2sts. **Next row:** p. Rep last 2 rows, with number of sts in brackets 4 more each time, until you have 48sts total.

Next k row: inc one st into first st, k22, inc one st into next 2sts, k22, inc one st into last st; [52sts]. Work 15 rows; [25 rows total].

Next row: k2 tog, k(22), k2 tog, k2 tog, k to last 2sts, k2 tog. **Next row:** p. Rep last 2 rows, with number of sts in brackets 2 less each time, until 40sts rem. Work 5 rows; [35 rows total].

Next row: k19, inc one st into next 2sts, k to end of row; [42sts].

Next k row: k(19), inc one st into next 4sts, k to end of row. **Next row:** p. Rep last 2 rows, with number of sts in brackets 2 more each time, until you have 54sts total. Work 3 rows; [45 rows total].

K2 tog at both ends of next and every foll k row until 48sts rem.

Next k row: k2 tog, k(20), k2 tog, k2 tog, k to last 2sts, k2 tog. **Next row:** p. Rep last 2 rows, with number of sts in brackets 2 less each time, until 32sts rem.

Next k row: k(14), k2 tog, k2 tog, k to end of row. **Next row:** p. Rep last 2 rows, with number of sts in brackets 1 less each time, until 26sts rem.

Next k row: (k2 tog, k2 tog, k5, k2 tog, k2 tog) twice; [18sts]. Work 9 rows; [75 rows total].

Next row: k2 tog, k2 tog, k to last 4sts, k2 tog, k2 tog; [14sts]. **Next row:** p. Cast off. This is the nose end.

Make up as for adult bear body and head.

LEGS
Make four, using dark brown
Cast on 10sts. This is the paw end.

Working in st-st throughout and beg with a k row, work 2 rows.

Next row: inc one st into first st, k(3), inc one st into next 2sts, k to last st, inc one st into last st. **Next row:** p. Rep last 2 rows, with number of sts in brackets 2 more each time, until you have 22sts total. Work 27 rows; [34 rows total]. Cast off.

Make up as for adult bear leg and ladderstitch to body.

Paw: About 5cm (2in) up from end of leg, bend paw up at right angles to leg and ladderstitch in position.

EARS
Make two, using dark brown
Cast on 20sts. Beg with a k row, st-st 6 rows.

Next row: (k2 tog, k6, k2 tog) twice; [16sts]. **Next row:** p. Cast off.

Make up as for adult bear ear and ladderstitch to head.

TAIL
Make one, using dark brown
Cast on 7sts. Working in st-st throughout and beg with a k row, work 4 rows.

K2 tog at both ends of next 2 k rows; [3sts]. **Next k row:** k3 tog. Break off yarn, slip end through rem st and pull tight. Hide end of yarn by sewing it back through knitting.

With smooth side outwards, sew tail piece to back of cub.

NOSE AND MOUTH FOR BOTH BEARS
With black yarn, make a few stitches on end of snout as a nose. Sew one stitch down from nose, and two big lines outwards from bottom of this stitch as a mouth. Secure yarn in smooth curve with tiny stitches worked in black thread (see Basic Techniques, p11).

BEAVER

Approximate size: 42cm (16½in) excluding tail

When a beaver builds its home, gnawing down small trees and dragging them into the river to build a watery shelter, it has a huge effect on its environment. Like a civil engineer, the beaver changes the look of its neighbourhood by creating a dam, a pool – even a new lake! The home (called a holt) is beautifully constructed, and can last for many centuries, added to over the years by a beaver's descendants. Perhaps you could encourage your child to build just such a sturdy home for their knitted beaver in the garden or park, created out of tree branches.

How easy is it to make?

Straightforward. The neck area on the body and head piece needs a little more concentration, with quite a lot of increasing in a short space.

Needles: 3¼mm (size 10, US 3)

Yarn: 100g chunky in brown; scraps of DK in black and white

Pair 14mm (½in) toy safety eyes

Tapestry and sewing needles

Black thread

Washable polyester toy stuffing

Tension

Over st-st, using 3¼mm (size 10, US 3) needles, 26sts and 34 rows to 10cm (4in).

Also . . .

Figures in [square brackets] give the total number of stitches or rows you should have at that stage.

All the information you need to work the Beaver is in Basic Techniques, p9–13.

BODY AND HEAD
Make one, using brown
Cast on 32sts. Working in st-st throughout and beg with a k row, work 2 rows.
Next row: inc one st into first 2sts, k(12), inc one st into next 4sts, k to last 2sts, inc one st into last 2sts. **Next row:** p. Rep last 2 rows, with number of sts in brackets 4 more each time, until you have 80sts total. Work 31 rows; [44 rows total].
Next row: k(38), k2 tog, k2 tog, k to end of row. Work 3 rows. Rep last 4 rows, with number of sts in brackets 1 less each time, until 60sts rem.
Next k row: (k4, inc one st into next 3sts) twice, k6, inc one st into next 3sts, k4, inc one st into next 6sts, k4, inc one st into next 3sts, k6, (inc one st into next 3sts, k4) twice; [84sts].
Next k row: k4, (inc one st into next 3sts, k8) three times, inc one st into next 3sts, k4, inc one st into next 3sts, (k8, inc one st into next 3sts) three times, k4; [108sts].Work 9 rows; [94 rows total].
Next row: (k10, k2 tog, k2 tog) four times, k10, (k2 tog, k2 tog, k10) three times; [94sts].
Next k row: k9, (k2 tog, k2 tog, k8) three times, k2 tog, k2 tog, (k8, k2 tog, k2 tog) three times, k9; [80sts]. **Next k row:** (k7, k2 tog, k2 tog) twice, (k6, k2 tog, k2 tog) three times, k6, (k2 tog, k2 tog, k7) twice; [66sts]. **Next k row:** (k5, k2 tog, k2 tog) three times, k4, k2 tog, k2 tog, k4, (k2 tog, k2 tog, k5) three times; [52sts]. **Next k row:** (k3, k2 tog, k2 tog) four times, k3, (k2 tog, k2 tog, k3) three times; [38sts]. **Next k row:** k2, (k2 tog, k2 tog, k1) three times, k2 tog, k2 tog, (k1, k2 tog, k2 tog) three times, k2; [24sts]. **Next row:** p. Cast off. This is the nose end.
With smooth sides outwards, fold body and head piece in half. Join nose end and long seam. Position and fit toy safety eyes, fill with stuffing then sew closed.

FRONT LEGS
Make two, using brown
Cast on 30sts. Working in st-st throughout and beg with a k row, work 16 rows.
K2 tog at both ends of next and every foll k row until 14sts rem. **Next row:** p. Cast off. This is the foot end.
With smooth sides outwards, fold leg piece in half. Join foot end and side seam. Fill with stuffing and sew closed. Ladderstitch to side of body.

BACK LEGS
Make two, using brown
Cast on 40sts. Working in st-st throughout and beg with a k row, work 20 rows.
K2 tog at both ends of next and every foll k row until 20sts rem. **Next row:** p. Cast off. This is the foot end.
Make up as for front leg and ladderstitch to body.

TAIL

Make one, using brown

Cast on 30sts. Working in st-st throughout and beg with a k row, work 60 rows.

K2 tog at both ends of next and every foll k row until 16sts rem. **Next row:** p. Cast off. Hide end of yarn by sewing it back through the knitting.

Sew cast on edge of tail to back of body.

EARS

Make two, using brown

Cast on 20sts. Working in st-st throughout and beg with a k row, work 8 rows.

Next row: (k2 tog, k6, k2 tog) twice; [16sts]. **Next k row:** (k2 tog, k4, k2 tog) twice; [12sts]. **Next row:** p. Cast off.

With smooth sides outwards, fold ear piece in half. Join around edge and sew to head.

NOSE AND MOUTH

Sew a few stitches in black yarn for nose. Work a big stitch straight down from nose, then two stitches outwards from base of first stitch. Secure yarn in smooth curves with tiny stitches worked in thread (see Basic Techniques, p11).

TEETH

Make one, using white

Cast on 8sts. Work in st-st throughout and beg with a k row, work 8 rows. K2 tog at both ends of next and every foll k row until 2sts rem. Break off yarn, slip end through rem sts and pull tight.

With smooth side outwards, sew tooth piece under mouth (see picture as guide). Sew a line of black thread up centre of teeth.

RACCOON

Approximate size: 34cm (13 1/2 in) excluding tail

Raccoons are mischievous animals, notorious as food thieves, garbage raiders and escape artists. Physically, they are quite unmistakable: a fox-like face with a black mask across the eyes, a stout cat-like build, a ringed tail and a characteristic rolling walk which makes them look as if they couldn't possibly climb into a trash can to delve for left-overs. This air of amiable innocence may be why young raccoons are often popular as pets. It's only when the raccoon matures that even the most devoted of owners may realise their mistake. The raccoon's insatiable curiosity, destructive nature and general untrustworthiness could try anyone's patience. So if there's chaos in your house after you've knitted this raccoon, you'll know who caused it . . . probably!

How easy is it to make?

Challenging. The pieces are straightforward to knit, but a few techniques are combined in this toy – colour changing, applying the eye patches, and embroidery on the ears.

Needles: 3 1/4mm (size 10, US 3)

Yarn: 100g DK in mid brown; 20g DK in brown mohair; 10g DK in white mohair; a small amount (less than 10g) DK in black

Pair 14mm (1/2 in) toy safety eyes

Tapestry and sewing needles

Black thread

Washable polyester toy stuffing

Tension

Over st-st, using 3 1/4mm (size 10, US 3) needles, 26sts and 34 rows to 10cm (4in).

Also . . .

Figures in [square brackets] give the total number of stitches or rows you should have at that stage.

All the information you need to work the Raccoon is in Basic Techniques, p9–13.

BODY AND HEAD
Make one, using white mohair and mid brown
Cast on 32sts in mid brown. Working in st-st throughout and beg with a k row, work 2 rows.

Next row: inc one st into first 2sts, k(12), inc one st into next 4sts, k to last 2sts, inc one st into last 2sts. **Next row:** p. Rep last 2 rows, with number of sts in brackets 4 more each time, until you have 56sts total.

Next k row: inc one st into first st, k26, inc one st into next 2sts, k to last st, inc one st into last st; [60sts]. Work 13 rows; [22 rows total].

Next row: k(28), k2 tog, k2 tog, k to end of row. Work 3 rows. Rep last 4 rows, with number of sts in brackets 1 less each time, until 44sts rem.

Next k row: k5, (inc one st into next 2sts, k6) twice, inc one st into next 2sts, (k6, inc one st into next 2sts) twice, k5; [54sts]. **Next k row:** k6, inc one st into next 2sts, k8, inc one st into next 2sts, k7, inc one st into next 4sts, k7, inc one st into next 2sts, k8, inc one st into next 2sts, k6; [66sts]. Work 13 rows; [68 rows total].

Next row: (k2 tog, k29, k2 tog) twice; [62sts]. **Next k row:** (k2 tog, k27, k2 tog) twice; [58sts].

Next k row: k2 tog, k2 tog, k(21), k2 tog four times, k to last 4sts, k2 tog, k2 tog. **Next row:** p. Rep last 2 rows, with number of sts in brackets 4 less each time, until 34sts rem. **Next row:** p.

Change to white mohair, next row: k2 tog, k(13), k2 tog, k2 tog, k to last 2sts, k2 tog. **Next row:** p. Rep last 2 rows, with number of sts in brackets 2 less each time, until 22sts rem.

Next k row: k2 tog, k to last 2sts, k2 tog. **Next row:** p. Rep last 2 rows. **Next k row:** k2 tog, k2 tog, k to last 4sts, k2 tog, k2 tog; [14sts]. **Next row:** p. Cast off. This is the nose end.

With smooth sides outwards, fold body and head piece in half. Join nose end and long seam (which runs along underside of raccoon). Fill with stuffing and sew closed.

FRONT LEGS
Make two, using mid brown
Cast on 28sts. Working in st-st throughout and beg with a k row, work 16 rows.
K2 tog at both ends of next and every foll k row until 12sts

rem. **Next row:** p. Cast off. This is the paw end.
With smooth sides outwards, fold leg piece in half. Join paw end and side seam, fill with stuffing then sew closed. Ladderstitch leg to side of body (see picture below as guide).

BACK LEGS
Make two, using mid brown
Cast on 36sts. Working in st-st throughout and beg with a k row, work 18 rows.
K2 tog at both ends of next and every foll k row until 14sts rem. **Next row:** p. Cast off. This is the paw end.
Make up as for front leg and ladderstitch to body.

EARS
Make four, using mid brown
Cast on 10sts. Working in st-st throughout and beg with a k row, work 10 rows.
K2 tog at both ends of next and every foll k row until 4sts rem. Next row: p. Cast off.
On two of the ear pieces, embroider long straight stitches in brown mohair, radiating out from centre of base of ear (see picture on p77 as guide). Match up ears in pairs and join around edge. Ladderstitch to head.
Make two 10cm (4in) lengths of single chain in white mohair and sew them to outer edges of ears.

TAIL
Make one, using brown mohair and mid brown
To work stripes, alternate yarn colour every 10 rows (see Basic Techniques, p10).
Cast on 30sts in mid brown. Working in st-st throughout and beg with a k row, work 76 rows.
Finish tail in brown mohair as follows. **Next row:** (k2 tog, k11, k2 tog) twice. **Next k row:** (k2 tog, k9, k2 tog) twice. **Next k row:** (k2 tog, k7, k2 tog) twice; [18sts].
Next row: p. Cast off.
With smooth sides outwards, fold tail piece in half. Join shaped end and long side seam. Fill with stuffing and sew closed. Ladderstitch tail to back of raccoon.

EYE PATCHES
Make two, using black
Cast on 4sts. P 1 row. Working in st-st throughout, next row: inc one st into first st, k2, inc one st into last st; [6sts]. Work 17 rows.
Next row: k2 tog, k2, k2 tog; [4sts]. **Next row:** p. Cast off.
Position and fit toy safety eye in eye patch, close to end (see picture below as guide). Sew eye patch to raccoon's face, pushing shank of eye into head.

FACE
Sew seven or eight stitches in black on end of snout as nose. Sew one long stitch in black as mouth. Secure yarn in smooth curve with tiny stitches worked in black thread. Between eye patches, embroider long straight stitches in black radiating out from nose (see picture on p77 as guide).

CLAWS
Sew three lines in black yarn on each paw for claws.

CHIPMUNK

Approximate size: 20cm (8in) excluding tail

A chipmunk is always on the move. It has tremendous energy and lives at great speed, constantly on the lookout with its bright little eyes for seeds and nuts to cram into its cheeks. It stores its food there until it can find a safe place to tuck into the feast. Or if there's excess food, the chipmunk will search out a hole to stash it as a reserve for the long winter months when food will be scarce.

How easy is it to make?

Challenging. The pieces are all easy to knit, in a single colour. Making up the chipmunk will take a little extra time, because of the embroidered stripes.

Needles: 3mm (size 11, US 2)

Yarn: 40g DK mohair in light brown; scraps of DK mohair in black, white, dark grey and mid grey; scraps of DK in pale pink and black

Pair 10mm (3/8in) toy safety eyes

Tapestry and sewing needles

Black thread

Washable polyester toy stuffing

Tension

Over st-st, using 3mm (size 11, US 2) needles, 28sts and 36 rows to 10cm (4in).

Also . . .

Figures in [square brackets] give the total number of stitches or rows you should have at that stage.

All the information you need to work the Chipmunk is in Basic Techniques, p9–13.

BODY AND HEAD
Make one, using light brown mohair
Cast on 20sts. Working in st-st throughout and beg with a k row, work 2 rows.

Next row: inc one st into first st, k7, inc one st into next 4sts, k to last st, inc one st into last st; [26sts]. **Next k row:** inc one st into first st, k10, inc one st into next 4sts, k to last st, inc one st into last st; [32sts]. **Next k row:** inc one st into first st, k14, inc one st into next 2sts, k to last st, inc one st into last st; [36sts]. Work 33 rows; [40 rows total].
Next row: k2 tog, k15, inc one st into next 2sts, k to last 2sts, k2 tog; [36sts]. **Next k row:** k2 tog, k2 tog, k13, inc one st into next 2sts, k13, k2 tog, k2 tog; [34sts]. **Next k row:** k2 tog, k2 tog, k12, inc one st into next 2sts, k to last 4sts, k2 tog, k2 tog; [32sts]. **Next k row:** k2 tog, k2 tog, k11, inc one st into next 2sts, k to last 4sts, k2 tog, k2 tog; [30sts]. **Next k row:** inc one st into first 2sts, (k5, inc one st into next 2sts) four times; [40sts]. **Next k row:** inc one st into first st, k8, inc one st into next 2sts, k18, inc one st into next 2sts, k8, inc one st into last st; [46sts]. Work 9 rows; [60 rows total].
Next k row: k2 tog, k(19), k2 tog, k2 tog, k to last 2sts, k2 tog. **Next row:** p. Rep last 2 rows, with number of sts in brackets 2 less each time, until 18sts rem. **Next row:** p. Cast off. This is the nose end.
With smooth sides outwards, fold body and head piece in half. Join nose end and long seam. Position and fit toy safety eyes, fill with stuffing then sew closed.

FRONT LEGS
Make two, using light brown mohair
Cast on 20sts. Working in st-st throughout and beg with a k row, work 10 rows.
****Next row:** (k2 tog, k6, k2 tog) twice; [16sts]. **Next k row:** (k2 tog, k4, k2 tog) twice; [12sts]. Work 13 rows; [26 rows total for front leg; 32 rows total for back leg]. **Next k row:** k1, k2 tog, k2 tog, k2, k2 tog, k2 tog, k1; [8sts]. **Next row:** p. Cast off. This is the paw end.
With smooth sides outwards, fold leg piece in half. Join end of paw and side seam, fill with stuffing then sew closed. Ladderstitch leg to front of body. Bend up a small paw at right angles to leg and ladderstitch in position (see Basic Techniques, p11, and picture opposite as guides).

BACK LEGS
Make two, using light brown mohair
Cast on 24sts. Working in st-st throughout and beg with a k row, work 14 rows.
Next row: (k2 tog, k8, k2 tog) twice; [20sts]. **Next row:** p. Work as for front leg from * to end.
Make up and sew paw as for front leg. Ladderstitch to body.

TAIL
Make one, using light brown mohair

Cast on 2sts. Working in st-st throughout and beg with a k row, work 2 rows.

Next row: inc one st into both sts; [4sts]. **Next k row:** inc one st into first st, k to last st, inc one st into last st. **Next row:** p. Rep last 2 rows; [8sts]. Work 98 rows; [106 rows total].

Next row: k2 tog, k4, k2 tog; [6sts]. **Next k row:** k2 tog, k2, k2 tog; [4sts]. **Next k row:** k2 tog, k2 tog; [2sts]. **Next row:** p2 tog. Break off yarn, slip end through rem st and pull tight.

With smooth sides outwards, fold tail piece in half, so narrow ends meet. Join tail around edge and ladderstitch short straight end to body. If tail looks puffy, sew a line of stitches down centre to make it lie flat.

EARS
Make two, using light brown mohair

Cast on 10sts. Working in st-st throughout and beg with a k row, work 6 rows.

Next row: (k2 tog, k1, k2 tog) twice; [6sts]. **Next row:** p. Cast off.

With smooth sides outwards, fold ear piece in half. Join around edge then sew to head.

STRIPES
With white mohair, work lines of chainstitch for stripes (see Basic Techniques, p10) as follows (using picture on p89 as guide). Start from nose end. Work line of chainstitch from point of nose, above eye, along side of head, along body, round sewn edge of tail, along second side of body and back along second side of head, above second eye and back to nose.

Work a second line of white close to first, this time going underneath eyes.

With black mohair, work lines of chainstitch on top of face stripes, on either sides of eyes.

With black mohair, work lines of chainstitch on either side of white stripe on body. Repeat with dark grey mohair. Using mid grey mohair, work final stripes close to the dark grey stripes, from base of tail up to end of nose.

NOSE AND MOUTH
With pink yarn, make a few stitches on end of snout as a nose. With black yarn work one big stitch for a mouth. Secure yarn in a smooth curve with tiny stitches worked in black thread (see Basic Techniques, p11).

MOOSE

Approximate size: 34cm (13½in)

The moose is a creature of habit, and has been studied by ecologists and economists for their mathematical precision in feeding patterns. The moose spends just the right length of time grazing for nutrient-rich water plants, and just enough time seeking out energy-filled land plants to keep its mighty frame healthy. Scientists are fascinated by the animals' ability to judge this daily balance enabling them to free up time to spend on other activities such as caring for their young.

How easy is it to make?

Challenging. A number of different techniques are combined in this toy. To mimic the real moose, the legs are long and spindly, needing to be supported inside by pipe-cleaners. So this toy isn't suitable for a very young child.

Needles: 3mm (size 11, US 2)

Yarn: 100g DK in mid brown; 20g DK in light brown; scraps of DK in dark brown

Pair 10mm (³/8in) toy safety eyes

Tapestry and sewing needles

Black thread

Four pipe-cleaners (optional)

Washable polyester toy stuffing

Tension

Over st-st, using 3mm (size 11, US 2) needles, 28sts and 36 rows to 10cm (4in).

Also . . .

Figures in [square brackets] give the total number of stitches or rows you should have at that stage.

All the information you need to work the Moose is in Basic Techniques, p9–13.

BODY, NECK AND HEAD
Make one, using mid brown
Cast on 28sts. P 1 row.

Next row: inc one st into first st, k(12), inc one st into next 2sts, k to last st, inc one st into last st. **Next row:** p. Rep last 2 rows, with number of sts in brackets 2 more each time, until you have 52sts total. Work 7 rows; [19 rows total].

Next row: k(24), k2 tog, k2 tog, k to end of row. **Next row:** p. Rep last 2 rows, with number of sts in brackets 1 less each time, until 44sts rem. Work 9 rows; [35 rows total].

Next row: k21, inc one st into next 2sts, k to end of row; [46sts]. **Next k row:** k22, inc one st into next 2sts, k to end of row; [48sts]. **Next k row:** k23, inc one st into next 2sts, k to end of row; [50sts]. Work 5 rows; [45 rows total].

Next row: k23, k2 tog, k2 tog, k to end of row; [48sts]. **Next k row:** k22, k2 tog, k2 tog, k to end of row; [46sts]. **Next k row:** k21, k2 tog, k2 tog, k to end of row; [44sts]. Work 3 rows; [53 rows total].

Next row: k2 tog, k to last 2sts, k2 tog. Work 3 rows. Rep last 4 rows until 24sts rem. Work 9 rows; [99 rows total].

Next row: inc one st into first 2sts, k to last 2sts, inc one st into last 2sts. **Next row:** p. Rep last 2 rows; [32sts]. Work 5 rows, [107 rows total]. K or p2 tog at both ends of next 3 rows.

Work 3 rows. **Next row:** k2 tog, k to last 2sts, k2 tog. Rep last 4 rows until 20sts rem.

Next k row: (k2 tog, k6, k2 tog) twice; [16sts]. **Next k row:** (k2 tog, k4, k2 tog) twice; [12sts]. **Next row:** p2 tog six times; [6sts]. Break off yarn, slip end through rem sts and pull tight. This is the nose end.

With smooth sides outwards, fold body, neck and head piece in half lengthways. Position and fit toy safety eyes about 7.5cm (3in) from nose end (see picture on p89 as guide). Join long seam, which will run down front of moose. Fill with stuffing through back end, then sew closed. (The moose now looks like a very long thin sock!)

Head: Bend head down at right angle to neck. Use ladderstitch to hold in position.

Neck: Bend neck upwards at shallow angle to body. Use ladderstitch to hold in position.

EARS
Make two, using mid brown
Cast on 14sts. Working in st-st throughout and beg with a k row, work 12 rows.

Next row: k(5), k2 tog, k2 tog, k to end of row. **Next row:** p. Rep last 2 rows, with number of sts in brackets 1 less each time, until 2sts rem. **Next k row:** k2 tog. Break off yarn, slip end through rem st and pull tight. Hide end of yarn by sewing it back through knitting.

With smooth sides outwards, fold ear piece in half. Sew base of ear to head, with open edges facing downwards (see picture on p89 as guide).

LEGS
Make four, using mid brown
Cast on 12sts. This is the hoof end.

Working in st-st throughout and beg with a k row, work 12 rows.

Inc one st at both ends of next and every foll alt k row until you have 26sts total. Work 17 rows; [54 rows total].

Next row: k2 tog, k(9), k2 tog, k2 tog, k to last 2sts, k2 tog. **Next row:** p. Rep last 2 rows, with number of sts in brackets 2 less each time, until 6sts rem. **Next row:** p. Cast off.

With smooth sides outwards, fold leg piece in half. Use ladderstitch to close end of hoof and side seam. Insert a pipe-cleaner to run full length of leg, fill with stuffing around pipe-cleaner and sew closed. Ladderstitch to body.

HORNS
Main branches, make two, using light brown
Cast on 20sts. Working in st-st throughout and beg with a k row, work 20 rows.

Next row: k2 tog ten times. **Next row:** p. Break off yarn, slip end through rem sts and pull tight.

With smooth sides outwards, fold main branch piece in half. Join around edge, then ladderstitch open end to side of head.

Small branches, make four, using light brown
Cast on 10sts. Working in st-st throughout and beg with a k row, work 6 rows. **Next row:** K2 tog five times. **Next row:** p. Break off yarn, slip end through rem sts and pull tight.

With smooth sides outwards, fold small branch piece in half. Join around edge, then ladderstitch open end to side of main branch (see picture on p89 as guide).

TAIL
Make one, using mid brown
Cast on 8sts. Working in st-st throughout and beg with a k row, work 6 rows.

Next row: k2 tog, k4, k2 tog. **Next row:** p. Cast off. Hide end of yarn by sewing it back through knitting.

With smooth side outwards, sew tail to back of moose.

NOSTRILS AND MOUTH
With dark brown yarn, make two or three stitches on either side of nose as nostrils. Use long straight stitches to make a mouth. Secure yarn in a smooth curve with tiny stitches worked in black thread (see Basic Techniques, p11, and picture on p89 as guides).

ON SAFARI

PARK RANGER

Approximate size: 29cm (11½in)

A park ranger on one of the great wildlife reserves of Africa has a tough job on his hands. Not only does he have to look after the animals that live on the land, but he must also keep a sharp eye out for poachers, who would like to kill elephants and rhinos for their valuable tusks and horns.

In a sandy-coloured uniform to camouflage him in the grasslands, and with binoculars to watch out for intruders, this park ranger is well-equipped to protect the animals who live under his care. He also has a wide-brimmed hat to protect his face from the baking sun, and a little knitted satchel – perhaps to collect samples of grasses and seeds, or perhaps to carry his lunch for his long days out in the bush!

How easy is it to make?

Straightforward. The pieces aren't complicated. The hat and jacket may take a little extra time to complete. If you're making this toy for a small child, you may want to sew the costume in place on the park ranger's body so that the pieces don't get lost.

Needles: 3 ¼mm (Size 10, US 3)

Yarn: 50g DK in dark brown; 70g DK in sandy brown; 20g DK in black; 20g DK in dark grey; scraps of DK in mid brown

Pair 10mm (³/₈in) toy safety eyes

Tapestry and sewing needles

Dark brown thread

Washable polyester toy stuffing

Three 10mm (³/₈in) diameter wooden beads

Props: cardboard, glue, tape, coloured beads, pipe cleaner and black paint for radio and binoculars; scraps of brown yarn and a small bead for satchel; silver paint

Tension

Over st-st, using 3 ¼mm (Size 10, US 3) needles, 26sts and 34 rows to 10cm (4in).

Also . . .

Figures in [square brackets] give the total number of stitches or rows you should have at that stage.

The Basic Person Pattern is on p12.

All the information you need to work the Park Ranger is in Basic Techniques, p9–13.

BODY AND HEAD
Make one, using sandy brown, dark grey and dark brown
Work as for Basic Person Pattern using the following colours: first 12 rows in sandy brown; next 3 rows in dark grey; rem rows in dark brown. Make up as for Basic Person Pattern.

LEGS
Make two, using dark grey and sandy brown
Work as for Basic Person Pattern using the following colours: first 22 rows in dark grey; rem rows in sandy brown. Make up as for Basic Person Pattern and ladderstitch to body.

ARMS AND EARS
Make two of each, using dark brown
Work and make up as for Basic Person Pattern and ladderstitch to body.

JACKET SLEEVES
Make two, using sandy brown
Cast on 26sts. K 2 rows.
Working in st-st throughout and beg with a k row, work 20 rows; [22 rows total].
K2 tog at both ends and once near middle of next and every foll k row until 11sts rem, ending with a k row. K 2 rows. Cast off.
With smooth sides outwards, fold sleeve piece in half and join side seam up to start of shaping.

JACKET RIGHT FRONT
Make one, using sandy brown
Cast on 14sts. K 2 rows. Working in st-st throughout and beg with a k row, work 22 rows; [24 rows total].
K2 tog at end of next and every foll k row until 8sts rem, ending with a k row. K 2 rows. Cast off.

JACKET LEFT FRONT
Make one, using sandy brown
Cast on 14sts. K 2 rows. Working in st-st throughout and beg with a k row, work 8 rows.
The next 2 rows will make the first buttonhole, near the edge of the jacket front.
First buttonhole row: *k to last 3sts. From left, imagine rem sts

are numbered 1, 2 & 3. K sts 3 and 2, pass st 3 over st 2 (cast it off), then k st 1.

Second buttonhole row: p2, turn and cast on one st, turn and p to end of row. Work 8 rows; [20 rows total].

To make the second buttonhole, rep first and second buttonhole rows.

Work 2 rows. K2 tog at beg of next and every foll k row until 10sts rem.

To make the third buttonhole, next k row: k2 tog, rep from * to end of first buttonhole row. Rep second buttonhole row.

Next row: k2 tog, k to end of row. K 2 rows. Cast off.

Sew around buttonholes using buttonhole stitch (see Basic Techniques, p10).

JACKET BACK

Make one, using sandy brown

Cast on 32sts. K 2 rows. Working in st-st throughout and beg with a k row, work 22 rows.

Next row: cast off 3sts, k to end of row; [29sts]. **Next row:** cast off 3sts, p to end of row; [26sts]. K2 tog at both ends of next and every foll k row until 14sts rem. K 2 rows. Cast off.

Lay jacket back with smooth side down. With smooth sides up, lay jacket left and right front pieces on top of jacket back, with long straight edges of front pieces overlapping in centre. Join side seams up to start of shaping. Position sleeves on either side of jacket and join sleeves to armholes of jacket.

JACKET POCKETS

Make two using sandy brown

Cast on 8sts. Beg with a k row, st-st 8 rows. Cast off.

Sew pockets to jacket front, leaving top edge open.

COLLAR

Make one, using sandy brown

Cast on 50sts. K 2 rows. Beg with a k row, st-st 4 rows. Cast off. Hide end of yarn by sewing it back through knitting.

With smooth side facing upwards, sew cast off edge of collar to top edge of jacket.

HAT BRIM

Make one, using sandy brown

Cast on 108sts. K 2 rows. Working in st-st and beg with a k row, **next row:** (k2 tog, k14, k2 tog) six times; [96sts].

Next k row: (k2 tog, k12, k2 tog) six times; [84sts]. **Next k row:** (k2 tog, k10, k2 tog) six times; [72sts]. **Next k row:** (k2 tog, k8, k2 tog) six times; [60sts]. **Next row:** p. Cast off.

Join short straight edges of brim to form full circle.

HAT TOP

Make one, using sandy brown

Cast on 60sts. Working in st-st throughout and beg with a k row, work 4 rows.

Next row: (k2 tog, k6, k2 tog) six times; [48sts]. **Next k row:** (k2 tog, k4, k2 tog) six times; [36sts]. **Next k row:** (k2 tog, k2, k2 tog) six times; [24sts]. **Next k row:** k2 tog twelve times; [12sts]. **Next row:** p. Break off yarn, slip end through rem sts and pull tight.

With smooth sides outwards, fold hat piece in half. Join side seam to form dome. Sew base of dome to inner edge of brim.

Work a line of running stitch (see Basic Techniques, p11) close to outer edge of brim in sandy brown yarn. Pull yarn gently to strengthen and straighten edge. Secure end of yarn by making a few stitches.

HAIR

Work as for Basic Person Pattern, using black.

MOUTH

Work as for Basic Person Pattern, using mid brown.

FINISHING TOUCHES

Radio: Stick eight rectangles of cardboard on top of each other. Between last two layers, sandwich length of pipe cleaner as an aerial, with end sticking out. Paint radio black, aerial silver and stick on beads as control knobs.

Binoculars: Roll up two rectangles of cardboard, tape them as tubes, then stick them together. Paint binoculars black and push four small circles of silver card up inside ends of tubes. Stick yarn to sides as hanging cords.

Satchel: On 3 $\frac{1}{4}$mm (Size 10, US 3) needles, cast on 12sts in brown yarn. Working in st-st throughout, work 30 rows. K2 tog at both ends of next and every foll k row until 2sts rem. Cast off. Use rem length of yarn to make loop, then secure end of yarn. Fold piece in three and join side seams.

Sew on a bead as fastener. Make shoulder strap from single chain of brown (see Basic Techniques, p10) and attach to sides of satchel.

ZEBRA

Approximate size: 23cm (9in)

Although there are lots of theories, no-one really knows why zebras have stripes. The unique pattern of each individual zebra may help them find each other amongst a huge herd. Or perhaps the stripes help the zebra to escape from being eaten, by dazzling and confusing the big cats that stalk them.

Some scientists, thinking that zebras might be attracted to anything striped, helping the herd to stick together, tested this theory by standing out in the plains holding boards painted with black and white stripes. Sure enough, zebras soon trotted over to take a look and join the strange new herd!

Whatever the reason for the zebras' striking markings, they are easy to reproduce in knitting – simply by changing yarn colour every few rows.

How easy is it to make?

Challenging. A number of techniques are combined in this toy – changing colour, shaping the body and head, and making pompoms. Beginners might like to try knitting this pattern in a single colour first, to make a horse, before progressing to a zebra.

Needles: 3mm (Size 11, US 2)

Yarn: 50g DK in black; 50g DK in white; scraps of DK in grey and dark brown

Pair 10mm (³/₈in) toy safety eyes

Tapestry needle

Washable polyester toy stuffing

Tension

Over st-st, using 3mm (Size 11, US 2) needles, 28sts and 36 rows to 10cm (4in).

Also . . .

Figures in [square brackets] give the number of stitches or rows you should have at that stage.

All the information you need to work the Zebra is in Basic Techniques, pages 9–13.

BODY, NECK AND HEAD
Make one, using white and black
To work stripes, alternate yarn colour every 4 rows (see Basic Techniques, page 10).
Cast on 28sts in black. P 1 row (first row of black).
Next row: inc one st into first st, k(12), inc one st into next 2sts, k to last st, inc one st into last st. **Next row:** p. Rep last 2 rows, with number of sts in brackets 2 more each time, until you have 52sts total. Work 7 rows; [19 rows total].
Next row: k(24), k2 tog, k2 tog, k to end of row. **Next row:** p. Rep last 2 rows, with number of sts in brackets 1 less each time, until 44sts rem. Work 9 rows; [35 rows total].
Next row: k21, inc one st into next 2sts, k to end of row; [46sts]. **Next k row:** k22, inc one st into next 2sts, k to end of row; [48sts]. **Next k row:** k23, inc one st into next 2sts, k to end of row; [50sts]. Work 5 rows; [45 rows total].
Next row: k23, k2 tog, k2 tog, k to end of row; [48sts]. **Next k row:** k22, k2 tog, k2 tog, k to end of row; [46sts]. **Next k row:** k21, k2 tog, k2 tog, k to end of row; [44sts]. Work 3 rows; [53 rows total].

Next row: k2 tog, k to last 2sts, k2 tog. Work 3 rows. Rep last 4 rows until 24sts rem. Work 9 rows [99 rows total].
Next row: inc one st into first 2sts, k to last 2sts, inc one st into last 2sts. **Next row:** p. Rep last 2 rows; [32sts]. Work 5 rows; [107 rows total]. K or p2 tog at both ends of next 3 rows.
Work 3 rows. **Next row:** k2 tog, k to last 2sts, k2 tog. Rep last 4 rows until 20sts rem.
To make black nose, cont in black – do not make any more stripes. **Next k row:** (k2 tog, k6, k2 tog) twice; [16sts]. **Next k row:** (k2 tog, k4, k2 tog) twice; [12sts]. **Next row:** p2 tog six times; [6sts]. Break off yarn, slip end through rem sts and pull tight.
With smooth sides outwards, fold body, neck and head piece in half lengthways.
Position and fit toy safety eyes in third stripe up from nose (see picture as guide). Starting at nose end, join long seam, which will run down front of zebra. Fill with stuffing through back end, then sew hole almost closed, leaving a 2.5cm (1in) hole. (The zebra now looks like a very long thin sock!)

Head: Bend head down at right angle to neck. Use ladderstitch to hold in position.

Neck: Bend neck upwards at shallow angle to body. Use ladderstitch to hold in position.

EARS

Make two, using black

Cast on 10sts.

Working in st-st throughout and beg with a k row, work 8 rows. **Next row:** k3, k2 tog, k2 tog, k3; [8sts]. **Next k row:** k2, k2 tog, k2 tog, k2; [6sts]. **Next k row:** k1, k2 tog, k2 tog, k1; [4sts]. **Next k row:** k2 tog, k2 tog; [2sts]. **Next k row:** k2 tog.

Break off yarn, slip end through rem st and pull tight. Hide end of yarn by sewing it back through knitting.

With smooth sides outwards, fold ear piece in half. Sew base of ear to head, with open edges facing forward (see picture as guide).

LEGS

Make four, using white and black

Cast on 12sts in black. Working in st-st throughout and beg with a k row, work 10 rows. This is the hoof.

Make rem of leg in stripes by alternating yarn colour every 4 rows as follows: Beg with a k row in white, work 2 rows. Inc one st at both ends of next and every foll alt k row until you have 26sts total. Work 13 rows; [50 rows total].

Next row: k2 tog, k(9), k2 tog, k2 tog, k to last 2sts, k2 tog. **Next row:** p. Rep last 2 rows, with number of sts in brackets 2 less each time, until 6sts rem. **Next row:** p. Cast off.

With smooth sides outwards, fold leg piece in half. Use ladderstitch to close end of hoof and side seam. Fill with stuffing and sew closed. Ladderstitch to body.

MANE

With a mixture of black and grey yarn, make five small pompoms (see Basic Techniques, p11). Sew them in a line along zebra's neck, then trim to make a neat mane.

TAIL

Cut forty 15cm (6in) lengths of black yarn and forty 15cm (6in) lengths of grey yarn. Mix them up so that colours are spread evenly. Tie all yarn together with a big knot at one end. Push this knot through hole at back of zebra. With black yarn, make a few stitches to close hole and secure tail.

NOSTRILS AND MOUTH

With dark brown yarn, make two or three stitches on either side of nose as nostrils. Use long straight stitches to make a mouth (see picture as guide).

THE LION FAMILY

Approximate size: Lion/Lioness 23cm (9in); Lion Cub 15cm (6in)

The lion is sometimes called 'king of the jungle', but they most often inhabit the deserts, open spaces and grasslands of Africa. Lions form strong family bonds and groups of lions, called 'prides', can contain many brothers and sisters from the same family. Lionesses will even give milk to cubs of other mothers, since they are all part of the family group. To strengthen family bonds, lions spend a lot of time grooming and playing with each other. The lionesses also hunt together, coordinating their attack so that the deer or zebra has little chance of escape.

These round-faced knitted lions don't look as if they'd be up to much zebra hunting. Their soft paws and cuddly bodies suit them more to lazing in the shade of a tree, keeping out of the hot African sun.

How easy is it to make?

Challenging. The legs, body and tail are all easy to make, with minimal shaping. The head and face need a little more concentration, with snout pieces that fold up and round to form the white face. The lion's mane may be a little more difficult for people who haven't made pom-poms before. The lioness and lion cub are more straightforward to make.

Tension

Over st-st, using 3¼mm (size 10, US 3) needles, 26sts and 34 rows to 10cm (4in).
Over st-st, using 3mm (size 11, US 2) needles, 28sts and 36 rows to 10cm (4in).

Also . . .

Figures in [square brackets] give the total number of stitches or rows you should have at that stage.

All the information you need to work the Lions is in Basic Techniques, p9–13.

For all lions

Pair 10mm (³/₈in) toy safety eyes

Tapestry and sewing needles

Black thread

Washable polyester toy stuffing

For a lion or lioness

Needles: 3 ¼mm (size 10, US 3)

Yarn: 80g DK in sandy brown; 50g DK in white; scraps of DK in dark brown (for lion, 10g DK in mid brown for mane)

For a lion cub

Needles: 3mm (size 11, US 2)

Yarn: 25g DK in sandy brown; 25g DK in white; scraps of DK in dark brown

LION

TOP OF BODY AND HEAD
Make one, using sandy brown
Cast on 14sts. Working in st-st throughout and beg with a k row, work 2 rows.

Next row: k(6), inc one st into next 2sts, k to end of row. **Next row:** p. Rep last 2 rows, with number of sts in brackets 1 more each time, until you have 30sts total. Work 21 rows; [38 rows total].

Next row: k(13), k2 tog, k2 tog, k to end of row. **Next row:** p. Rep last 2 rows, with number of sts in brackets 1 less each time, until 22sts rem.

Next k row: k10, inc one st into next 2sts, k10; [24sts]. **Next k row:** k11, inc one st into next 2sts, k11; [26sts]. **Next k row:** k12, inc one st into next 2sts, k12; [28sts]. Work 7 rows; [58 rows total].

Next row: k12, k2 tog, k2 tog, k12; [26sts] **Next k row:** k11, k2 tog, k2 tog, k11; [24sts].

Next k row: k10, k2 tog, k2 tog, k10; [22sts]. **Next row:** p. Cast off. This is the head end.

BASE OF BODY AND HEAD
Make one, using white
Work as for top of head and body to end, but do not cast off. Mark both ends of last row with coloured yarn.

Next row: cast on 8sts, k9, k2 tog, k2 tog, k to end of row. **Next row:** cast on 8sts, p to end of row.

Next row: k2 tog, k(14), k2 tog, k2 tog, k to last 2sts, k2 tog. **Next row:** p. Rep last 2 rows, with number of sts in brackets 2 less each time, until 20sts rem. Work 5 rows; [14 rows total from marker].

Next row: k6, k2 tog four times, k6; [16sts]. **Next k row:** k4, k2 tog four times, k4; [12sts]. **Next row:** p. Cast off. This is the nose end.

With smooth sides outwards, join base and top pieces along one straight seam. Match head end of sandy piece with coloured marker on white piece. Rep on other side of lion. Join tops of two flaps forming lion's snout. Position and fit toy safety eyes. Fold top edge of snout up to head and sew in place. Fill snout, head and body with stuffing, then sew closed. Remove coloured markers.

LEGS
Make four, using sandy brown
Cast on 12sts. This is the paw end. Working in st-st throughout and beg with a k row, work 2 rows.

Next row: inc one st into first st, k(4), inc one st into next 2sts, k to last st, inc one st into last st. **Next row:** p. Rep last 2 rows, with number of sts in brackets 2 more each time, until you have 28sts total. Work 29 rows; [38 rows total].

K2 tog at both ends and once near middle of next and every foll k row until 16sts rem. **Next row:** p. Cast off.

With smooth sides outwards, fold leg piece in half. Join end of paw and long side seam. Fill with stuffing, then sew closed and ladderstitch to body.

About 4cm (1½in) from end, bend paw up at right angles to leg and ladderstitch in position (see picture as guide).

TAIL
Make one, using sandy brown
Cast on 14sts. Working in st-st throughout and beg with a k row, work 26 rows.

Next row: k2 tog seven times; [7sts]. Break off yarn, slip end through rem sts and pull tight.

With smooth sides outwards, fold tail piece in half. Join side seam, fill with stuffing and ladderstitch open end to body. With a mixture of sandy brown and mid brown yarn, make a small shaggy pom-pom (see Basic Techniques, p11). Sew to end of tail.

EARS
Make two, using sandy brown
Cast on 20sts. Working in st-st throughout and beg with a k row, work 6 rows.

Next row: (k2 tog, k6, k2 tog) twice; [16sts]. **Next k row:** (k2 tog, k4, k2 tog) twice; [12sts]. **Next row:** p. Cast off.

With smooth sides together, fold ear piece in half. Join around edge, then ladderstitch to head.

NOSE, MOUTH AND CLAWS
With black yarn, make two or three stitches on end of snout for nose. Sew one stitch down from nose, and two big lines outwards from bottom of this stitch as a mouth. Secure yarn in a smooth curve with tiny stitches worked in black thread (see Basic Techniques, p11). Sew three big stitches on each paw for claws.

MANE
With a mixture of sandy brown and mid brown yarn, make seven or eight large shaggy pom-poms. Sew them on top of the lion's head (see picture on p98 as guide). Trim slightly to neaten.

LIONESS

Work as for lion, but do not make mane.

LION CUB

Note: The cub is worked using size 3mm (size 11, US 2) needles.

TOP OF BODY AND HEAD
Make one, using sandy brown
Cast on 10sts. Working in st-st throughout and beg with a k row, work 2 rows.

Next row: k(4), inc one st into next 2sts, k to end of row. **Next row:** p. Rep last 2 rows, with number of sts in brackets 1 more each time, until you have 20sts total. Work 15 rows; [26 rows total].

Next row: k(8), k2 tog, k2 tog, k to end of row. **Next row:** p. Rep last 2 rows, with number of sts in brackets 1 less each time, until 14sts rem. **Next k row:** k6, inc one st into next 2sts, k6; [16sts]. **Next k row:** k7, inc one st into next 2sts, k7; [18sts]. Work 5 rows; [40 rows total].

Next row: k7, k2 tog, k2 tog, k7; [16sts]. **Next k row:** k6, k2 tog, k2 tog, k6; [14sts]. **Next row:** p. Cast off. This is the head end.

BASE OF BODY AND HEAD
Make one, using white
Work as for top of body and head, but do not cast off. Mark both ends of last row with coloured yarn.

Next row: cast on 7sts, k5, k2 tog, k2 tog, k5; [19sts]. **Next row:** cast on 7sts, p to end of row; [26sts].

Next row: k2 tog, k(9), k2 tog, k2 tog, k to last 2sts, k2 tog. **Next row:** p. Rep last 2 rows, with number of sts in brackets 2 less each time, until 14sts rem. Work 3 rows.

Next row: k3, k2 tog four times, k3; [10sts]. **Next k row:** k1, k2 tog four times, k1; [6sts]. **Next row:** p. Cast off. This is the nose end. Make up as for lion body and head.

LEGS
Make four, using sandy brown
Cast on 10sts. Working in st-st throughout and beg with a k row, work 2 rows.

Next row: inc one st into first st, k(3), inc one st into next 2sts, k to last st, inc one st into last st. **Next row:** p. Rep last 2 rows, with number of sts in brackets 2 more each time, until you have 22sts total. Work 23 rows; [30 rows total].

K2 tog at both ends and once near middle of next and every foll k row until 13sts rem. **Next row:** p. Cast off.

Make up as for lion and ladderstitch to body. Make paws as for lion paws, making bend at 2.5cm (1in) from end of leg.

TAIL
Make one, using sandy brown
Cast on 10sts. Working in st-st throughout and beg with a k row, work 16 rows.

Next row: k2 tog five times; [5sts]. Break off yarn, slip end through rem sts and pull tight.

Make up as for lion tail and ladderstitch to back of body sewing a small pom-pom to end of tail.

EARS
Make two, using sandy brown
Cast on 14sts. Beg with a k row, st-st 4 rows.

Next row: (k2 tog, k3, k2 tog) twice; [10sts]. **Next row:** p. Cast off.

Make up as for lion ears and ladderstitch to head.

RHINOCEROS

Approximate size: 38cm (15in)

The few rhinos that exist today are remnants of a past when many vast plant-eating creatures walked the earth.

Rhinos have very bad eyesight. If you were to stand absolutely still, only about thirty metres away from one, you would not be noticed at all. However, a rhino's sense of smell is excellent, since its smell-detector is bigger than its brain! Under the wrinkles in a rhinoceros's skin lurk many irritating pests and insects. But luckily, rhinos have developed a helpful partnership with birds called oxpeckers, who busily search out the bugs and get a free meal for their services.

For this knitted toy, the wrinkled, 'armour-plated' effect of the rhino's skin has been re-created using separate panels of knitting sewn on to the body.

How easy is it to make?

Challenging. This toy combines a few techniques, and the body and legs are all knitted as one piece. This pattern is probably best suited to a more experienced knitter.

Needles: 3 3/4mm (size 9, US 4)

Yarn: 120g DK in grey; scraps of DK in white and black

Pair 14mm (1/2 in) toy safety eyes

Tapestry needle

Washable polyester toy stuffing

Tension

Over st-st, using 3 3/4 mm (size 9, US 4) needles, 18sts and 28 rows to 10cm (4in).

Also . . .

Figures in [square brackets] give the total number of stitches or rows you should have at that stage.

All the information you need to work the Rhino is in Basic Techniques, p9–13.

LEGS AND BODY
Make two, using grey

Cast on 20sts. Working in st-st throughout and beg with a k row, work 20 rows.

Next row: cast off 10sts. Break off yarn. This is the first leg – leave rem sts on needle.

To make second leg, cast on 20sts on to needle which holds first leg. Beg with a k row, work 20 rows on these 20sts.

Next row: cast off 10sts, k across rem 10sts. Turn and cast on 15sts, then turn and k across rem 10sts of first leg. **Next row:** p across all 35sts. The legs are now joined together.

Next row: inc one st into first 2sts, k to last 2sts, inc one st into last 2sts. **Next row:** p. Rep last 2 rows until you have 51sts total. Mark both ends of this row with coloured yarn. Work 27 rows; [35 rows total from cast on edge between legs].

Rem part of body is worked as two sections, to give shoulder and back humps, as follows:
Next row: k2 tog, k14, k2 tog, k2 tog. Turn and p back across these 17sts. **Next row:** k2 tog, k11, k2 tog, k2 tog.

Turn and p back across these 14sts as follows: p2 tog, p10, p2 tog. **Next row:** k2 tog, k2 tog, k4, k2 tog, k2 tog. Turn and cast off these 8sts. Break off yarn.

With smooth side of work facing, rejoin yarn and cast off until 20sts rem. Cont in k, k2 tog, k2 tog, k14, k2 tog; [17sts].

Next k row: k2 tog, k2 tog, k11, k2 tog; [14sts]. **Next row:** p2 tog, p10, p2 tog; [12sts]. **Next row:** k2 tog, k2 tog, k4, k2 tog, k2 tog; [8sts]. Cast off.

With smooth sides outwards, fold leg sections in half and join leg side seams.

FOOTPADS
Make four, using grey

Cast on 4sts. Working in st-st throughout and beg with a k row, work 2 rows.

Next row: inc one st into first st, k2, inc one st into last st; [6sts]. Work 10 rows; [13 rows total]. **Next row:** p2 tog, p2, p2 tog; [4sts]. **Next row:** k. Cast off.

Cover bottom of leg with footpad and sew in place. Fill leg with stuffing. Rep for other three legs.

GUSSET

Make one, using grey

Cast on 3sts. Working in st-st throughout and beg with a k row, work 2 rows.

Inc one st at both ends of next and every foll k row until you have 13sts total. Work 47 rows; [58 rows total]. K2 tog at both ends of next and every foll k row until 3sts rem. **Next row:** p. Cast off.

Join one pointed end of gusset to body piece at coloured marker. Join one side of gusset to body as follows: Stitch from gusset point down to first leg. Cont, stitching gusset to unfinished edge of first leg, then along straight edge between legs (see below). Cont along unfinished edge of second leg and up to match second gusset point with second marker; rep to join second body piece to other side of gusset.

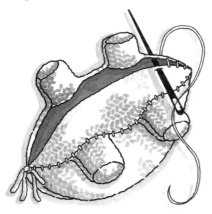

Starting at first marker, join body pieces along back of rhinoceros. Cont until approx 10cm (4in) from second marker. Fill body with stuffing, then sew closed. Remove markers.

HEAD

Make one, using grey

Cast on 44sts. Working in st-st throughout and beg with a k row, work 4 rows.

Next row: k16, inc one st into next st, k10, inc one st into next st, k16; [46sts]. **Next row:** p17, inc one st into next st, p10, inc one st into next st, p17; [48sts]. **Next row:** k18, inc one st into next st, k10, inc one st into next st, k18; [50sts]. **Next row:** p19, inc one st into next st, p10, inc one st into next st, p19; [52sts]. **Next row:** k20, inc one st into next st, k10, inc one st into next st, k20; [54sts]. **Next row:** p21, inc one st into next st, p10, inc one st into next st, p21; [56sts]. **Next row:** inc one st into first st, k21, inc one st into next st, k10, inc one st into next st, k21, inc one st into last st; [60sts]. **Next row:** inc one st into first st, p23, inc one st into next st, p10, inc one st into next st, p23, inc one st into last st; [64sts]. Work 6 rows; [18 rows total].

Next row: k2 tog, k(23), k2 tog, k10, k2 tog, k to last 2sts, k2 tog. **Next row:** p. Rep last 2 rows, with number of sts in brackets 2 less each time until 32sts rem. Work 7 rows; [40 rows total].

Next row: k2 tog, k6, (k2 tog, k2) four times, k6, k2 tog; [26sts]. **Next k row:** k2 tog, k4, (k2 tog, k2) four times, k2, k2 tog; [20sts]. **Next row:** p8, p2 tog, p2 tog, p8; [18sts]. Cast off. This is the nose end.

With smooth sides outwards, fold head piece in half. Join nose end and side seams and fill with stuffing. Ladderstitch open end to front of body.

BIG HORN

Make one, using white

Cast on 12sts. Working in st-st throughout and beg with a k row, work 6 rows.

Next row: inc one st into first st, k3, k2 tog, k2 tog, k3, inc one st into last st; [12sts]. **Next row:** p. Rep last 2 rows.

*Next row: k4, k2 tog, k2 tog, k4; [10sts]. **Next row:** p3, p2 tog, p2 tog, p3; [8sts]. **Next row:** k2 tog four times; [4sts]. **Next row:** p2 tog, p2 tog; [2sts]. **Next row:** k2 tog. Break off yarn, slip end through rem st and pull tight.

With smooth sides outwards, fold horn piece in half. Join side seam and fill with stuffing. Ladderstitch open end to top of nose (see picture as guide).

SMALL HORN

Make one, using white

Cast on 12sts. Beg with a k row, st-st 2 rows.

Next row: inc one st into first st, k3, k2 tog, k2 tog, k3, inc one st into last st; [12sts]. **Next row:** p. Work as for big horn from * to end.

Make up as for big horn and ladderstitch to nose.

SHOULDER PATCH

Make one, using grey

Cast on 10sts. *Working in st-st throughout and beg with a k row, work 2 rows. Inc one st at both ends of next and every foll k row until you have 16sts total. Work 29 rows; [36 rows total first time round; 78 rows total second time round]. K2 tog at both ends of next and every foll k row until 10sts remain. **Next row:** p.** Rep once from * to **, then cast off.

Lay patch at right angles across rhino's shoulders, with central narrow portion lined up with shoulder seam. Sew across patch along line of shoulder seam. Join half of patch to body with ladderstitch, enclosing a little stuffing to make it bulge. Rep for other half of patch.

BOTTOM PATCH

Make one, using grey

Cast on 14sts. #Working in st-st throughout and beg with a k row, work 2 rows. Inc one st at both ends of next and every foll k row until you have 20sts total. Work 29 rows; [36 rows total first time round; 78 rows total second time round]. K2 tog at both ends of next and every foll k row until 14sts remain. **Next row:** p.## Rep once from # to ##, then cast off.

Attach bottom patch as for shoulder patch, across back of rhino (see picture as guide).

EARS

Make two, using grey

Cast on 10sts. Working in st-st throughout and beg with a k row, work 4 rows.

Next row: inc one st into first st, k3, inc one st into next 2sts, k3, inc one st into last st; [14sts]. **Next k row:** inc one st into first st, k5, inc one st into next 2sts, k5, inc one st into last st; [18sts]. Work 5 rows; [12 rows total].

Next row: (k2 tog, k5, k2 tog) twice; [14sts]. **Next k row:** (k2 tog, k3, k2 tog) twice; [10sts]. **Next k row:** (k2 tog, k1, k2 tog) twice; [6sts]. **Next k row:** k2 tog three times; [3sts].

Next k row: k3 tog. Break off yarn, slip end through rem st and pull tight.

With smooth sides outwards, fold ear piece in half. Join around edge then sew to head.

TAIL

Make one, using grey

Cast on 12sts. Working in st-st throughout and beg with a k row, work 24 rows.

Next row: (k2, k2 tog, k2) twice; [10sts]. **Next k row:** (k2, k2 tog) twice, k2; [8sts]. **Next k row:** k2, k2 tog, k2 tog, k2; [6sts]. **Next k row:** k2 tog three times; [3sts]. **Next k row:** k3 tog. Break off yarn, slip end through rem st and pull tight.

With smooth sides outwards, fold tail piece in half. Join around edge and ladderstitch to back of body.

NOSTRILS AND MOUTH

With black yarn, make three stitches on either side of nose as nostrils. Use long straight stitches to make a mouth (see Basic Techniques, p11, and picture as guides).

ELEPHANT

Approximate size: 40cm (16in) excluding tail

Elephants are the largest animals that live on land, and they live for a very long time – often seventy years or more. They spend their days in caring family groups, are intelligent and sensitive and have a very impressive ability to learn and remember.

The elephant's trunk is strong enough to rip up trees and yet sensitive enough to pick up small objects like leaves and grasses. An elephant can also give itself a shower by filling its trunk at a watering hole, then spraying the water over its head. The trunk is used to smell, to drink, and to pick things up to eat. In fact, the reason why the trunk developed was because without it, elephants wouldn't be able to reach food on the ground!

Maybe this knitted elephant's trunk won't be strong enough to rip up trees, but the impressive tusks and intelligent face will be a reminder of his huge relations roaming the African plains.

How easy is it to make?

Challenging. The body and legs are all knitted as one piece, and the head and trunk are quite an unusual pattern. This project is best suited to a more experienced knitter.

Needles: 3 3/4mm (size 9, US 4)

Yarn: 150g DK in grey; scraps of DK in white

Pair 14mm (1/2 in) toy safety eyes

Tapestry needle

Washable polyester toy stuffing

Tension

Over st-st, using 3 3/4mm (size 9, US 4) needles, 18sts and 28 rows to 10cm (4in).

Also . . .

Figures in [square brackets] give the total number of stitches or rows you should have at that stage.

All the information you need to work the Elephant is in Basic Techniques, p9–13.

LEGS AND BODY
Make two, using grey
Cast on 30sts. Working in st-st throughout and beg with a k row, work 18 rows.
Next row: cast off 15sts, k to end of row. Break off yarn. This is the first leg – leave rem sts on needle.
To make second leg, on empty needle, cast on 30sts. Begin with a k row, work 18 rows. **Next row:** cast off 15sts, k to end of row.
Next row: p15 across second leg, turn and cast on 15sts, turn and p15 across first leg; [45sts]. The legs are now joined together. Work 2 rows.
Next row: inc one st into first st, k(13), inc one st into next st, k15, inc one st into next st, k to last st, inc one st into last st. **Next row:** p. Rep last 2 rows, with number of sts in brackets 2 more each time, until you have 69sts total.

Mark both ends of this row with coloured yarn. Work 9 rows; [22 rows total from cast on edge between legs].
Next row: k(25), k2 tog, k15, k2 tog, k to end of row. **Next row:** p. Rep last 2 rows, with number of sts in brackets 1 less each time, until 59sts rem. Work 3 rows; [34 rows total from cast on edge between legs].
K2 tog at both ends of next and every foll k row until 45sts rem. **Next row:** k2 tog, k2 tog, k to last 4sts, k2 tog, k2 tog. **Next row:** p2 tog, cast off to last 2sts, p2 tog. Break off yarn, slip end through rem st and pull tight.
With smooth sides outwards, fold leg sections in half and join leg side seams.

FOOTPADS
Make four, using grey
Cast on 6sts. P1 row. Working in st-st throughout, next row: inc one st into first st, k4, inc one st into last st. **Next row:** inc one st into first st, p6, inc

one st into last st. Work 14 rows; [17 rows total].
Next row: k2 tog, k6, k2 tog.
Next row: p2 tog, p4, p2 tog.
Next row: k. Cast off.
Cover bottom of leg with footpad and sew in place. Fill leg with stuffing. Rep for other three legs.

BODY GUSSET
Make one, using grey
Cast on 3sts. P 1 row. Working in st-st throughout, inc one st at both ends of next and every foll k row until you have 17sts total. Work 73 rows; [87 rows total]. K2 tog at both ends of next and every foll k row until 3sts rem. **Next row:** p. Cast off.
Attach gusset as for rhino, then complete body as for rhino (see p101).

HEAD AND TRUNK
Make one, using grey
Cast on 46sts. Working in st-st throughout and beg with a k row, work 8 rows. **Next row:** inc one st into first st, k6, inc one st into next st, k7, inc one st into next st, k6, inc one st into next 2sts, k6, inc one st into next st, k7, inc one st into next st, k6, inc one st into last st, [54sts].
Next k row: inc one st into first st, (k7, inc one st into next 2sts) five times, k7, inc one st into last st; [66sts]. Work 33 rows; [44 rows total].
Next row: k6, (k2 tog, k3) three times, k2 tog, k20, (k2 tog, k3) three times, k2 tog, k6; [58sts]. **Next k row:** k6, k2 tog seven times, k18, k2 tog seven times, k6; [44sts]. **Next k row:** k2 tog, k4, k2 tog four times, k16, k2 tog four times, k4, k2 tog; [34sts]. Work 3 rows; [52 rows total].
K2 tog at both ends of next and every foll alt k row until 12sts rem. Work 15 rows; [108 rows total]. Cast off.
With smooth sides outwards, fold head and trunk piece in half. Join end of trunk and long side seam, to neck. Position and fit toy safety eyes (see diagram below as guide). Fill with stuffing and ladderstitch open end of neck to body. Bend trunk downwards at right angle to head (see picture on p92–93 as guide). Ladderstitch in position (see diagram below).

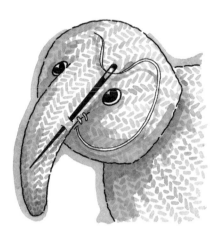

EARS
Make two each of pieces A and B, using grey
Piece A – Cast on 15sts. P 1 row. Working in st-st throughout, next row: inc one st into first 2sts, k to last 2sts, inc one st into last 2sts. Next row: inc one st into first 2sts, p to last 2sts, inc one st into last 2sts. Rep last 2 rows; [31sts].
Next row: inc one st into first st, k to last st, inc one st into last st. **Next row:** inc one st into first st, p to last st, inc one st into last st; [35sts]. Work 9 rows; [16 rows total].
Next row: p2 tog, p to last 2sts, p2 tog; [33sts]. **Next row:** k2 tog, k2 tog, k to last 4sts, k2 tog, k2 tog; [29sts]*. **Next row:** cast off 15sts, p2 tog, p2 tog, p to last 2sts, p2 tog; [11sts]. **Next row:** k2 tog, k to last 4sts, k2 tog, k2 tog; [8sts]. **Next row:** p2 tog, p2 tog, p2, p2 tog; [5sts]. **Next row:** k2 tog, k1, k2 tog; [3sts]. **Next row:** p2 tog, p1; [2sts]. Break off yarn, slip end

through rem sts and pull tight.
Piece B – Work as for Piece A to *. **Next row:** p2 tog, p to last 19sts, p2 tog, p2 tog, cast off to end of row; [11sts rem]. Break off yarn. With smooth sides facing, rejoin yarn.
Next row: k2 tog, k2 tog, k to last 2sts, k2 tog; [8sts]. **Next row:** p2 tog, p2, p2 tog, p2 tog; [5sts]. **Next row:** k2 tog, k1, k2 tog; [3sts]. **Next row:** p1, p2 tog; [2sts]. Break off yarn, slip end through rem sts and pull tight.
With smooth sides outwards, match up ear pieces in pairs. Join around edge and ladderstitch to side of head.

TUSKS
Make two, using white
Cast on 12sts. Working in st-st throughout and beg with a k row, work 8 rows.
Next row: inc one st into first st, k3, k2 tog, k2 tog, k3, inc one st into last st. **Next row:** p. Rep last 2 rows twice more; [12sts].
Next k row: k(4), k2 tog, k2 tog, k to end of row. **Next row:** p. Rep last 2 rows, with number of sts in brackets 1 less each time, until 4sts rem. **Next k row:** k2 tog, k2 tog. **Next row:** p. Cast off.
With smooth sides outwards, fold tusk piece in half. Join side seam, fill with stuffing then ladderstitch open end to cheek. Make extra stitches to hold tusk to side of trunk.

TAIL
Cut six 20cm (8in) lengths of grey yarn. Holding lengths in a bunch, tie in middle with another piece of grey yarn (use this later to attach tail). Fold lengths of yarn in half and divide ends into three groups of four. Plait groups together until 5cm (2in) from end (see Basic Techniques, p11). Tie end of tail in knot, and sew to body.

WARTHOG

Approximate size: 30cm (12in) excluding tail

Although the warthog's prominent tusks look fierce and unfriendly, it's far more likely that a warthog would run away from you than launch an attack.

While other types of pig-like creatures have often been bred by people to become farm animals, the warthog has stubbornly refused to be tamed. Living in the grasslands of Africa, its only contact with farmers is when it occasionally sneaks on to farmland to steal food. It's always on the look-out for a free lunch.

This knitted warthog seems to be no exception. With his shiny little eyes and nimble trotters, he looks like he might be just as cheeky and greedy as his African cousins.

How easy is it to make?

Challenging. This toy combines a few techniques and has quite a lot of pieces to knit. This pattern is best suited to a more experienced knitter.

Needles: 3 3/4mm (Size 9, US 4)

Yarn: 140g DK in russet; scraps of DK in white and black

Pair 14mm (1/2 in) toy safety eyes

Tapestry and sewing needles

Black thread

Washable polyester toy stuffing

Tension

Over st-st, using 3 3/4mm (size 9, US 4) needles, 18sts and 28 rows to 10cm (4in).

Also . . .

Figures in [square brackets] give the total number of stitches or rows you should have at that stage.

All the information you need to work the Warthog is in Basic Techniques, p9–13.

BODY AND HEAD
Make one, using russet
Cast on 24sts. P 1 row. Working in st-st throughout, next row: k1, inc one st into next 2sts, k(6), inc one st into next 2sts, k2, inc one st into next 2sts, k to last 3sts, inc one st into next 2sts, k1. **Next row:** p. Rep last 2 rows, with number of sts in brackets 4 more each time, until you have 72sts total.

Next k row: (k1, inc one st into next st, k32, inc one st into next st, k1) twice. [76sts] Work 15 rows; [29 rows total].

Next row: k1, k2 tog, k(32), k2 tog, k2, k2 tog, k to last 3sts, k2 tog, k1. **Next row:** p. Rep last 2 rows, with number of sts in brackets 2 less each time, until 60sts rem. Work 7 rows; [43 rows total].

Next row: k28, inc one st into next st, k2, inc one st into next st, k to end of row; [62sts].

Next k row: k(28), inc one st into next 2sts, k2, inc one st into next 2sts, k to end of row.

Next row: p. Rep last 2 rows, with number of sts in brackets 2 more each time, until you have 78sts total. Work 3 rows; [55 rows total].

K or p2 tog at both ends of next 3 k rows; [72sts].

Next k row: k2 tog, k(31), k2 tog, k2, k2 tog, k to last 2sts, k2 tog. **Next row:** p. Rep last 2 rows, with number of sts in brackets 2 less each time, until 48sts rem.

Next k row: k(21), k2 tog, k2, k2 tog, k to end of row. **Next row:** p. Rep last two rows, with number of sts in brackets 1 less each time, until 30sts rem. Work 5 rows; [95 rows total]. Cast off. This is the snout end.

With smooth sides outwards, fold body and head piece in half and join long seam. Fill with stuffing and sew back end closed, leaving snout end open.

SNOUT
Make one, using russet
Cast on 11sts. P 1 row. Working in st-st throughout, next row: inc one st into first st, k9, inc one st into last st. Work 3 rows.

Next row: k2 tog, k to last 2sts, k2 tog; [11sts]. Cast off.
Cover snout hole in head with snout piece and sew in position.

FRONT LEGS

Make two, using russet

Cast on 20sts. Working in st-st throughout and beg with a k row, work 14 rows.

Inc one st at both ends of next and every foll alt k row until you have 28sts total. Work 5 rows; [32 rows total].

Next row: cast off 14sts, k to end of row; [14sts]. K2 tog at both ends of next and every foll k row until 8sts rem. **Next row:** p2 tog, p to last 2sts, p2 tog; [6sts]. Cast off.

With smooth sides outwards, fold leg piece in half. Join narrow end and side seam, and fill with stuffing. Sew a 2.5cm (1in) line of stitches up centre of foot, at right angles to base of foot, forming trotter. Ladderstitch open end of leg to body.

BACK LEGS

Make two, using russet

Cast on 20sts. Working in st-st throughout and beg with a k row, work 14 rows.

Inc one st at both ends of next and every foll alt k row until you have 28sts total. Work 3 rows. Inc one st into first and last 2sts of next and every foll alt k row until you have 36sts total. Work 5 rows; [38 rows total].

Next row: cast off 18sts, k to end of row. K2 tog at both ends of next and every foll k row until 8sts rem. **Next p row:** p2 tog, p to last 2sts, p2 tog; [6sts]. Cast off.

Make up as for front legs and ladderstitch to body.

EARS

Make two each of pieces A and B, using russet

Piece A – Cast on 5sts. Working in st-st throughout and beg with a k row, work 4 rows.

Next row: inc one st into first 2sts, k2, inc one st into last st. **Next k row:** inc one st into first 2sts, k to end of row. Work 7 rows; [14 rows total]. **Next row:** k to last 2sts, k2 tog. Next k row: k7, k2 tog. **Next k row:** k6, k2 tog. K2 tog at both ends of next 2 k rows; [3sts]. Cast off.

Piece B – Cast on 5sts. Working in st-st throughout and beg with a k row, work 4 rows.

Next k row: inc one st into first st, k2, inc one st into last 2sts. **Next k row:** k to last 2sts, inc one st into last 2sts. Work 7 rows. **Next row:** k2 tog, k to end of row. **Next k row:** k2 tog, k7. **Next k row:** k2 tog, k6. K2 tog at both ends of next 2 k rows. Cast off.

With smooth sides outwards, match up ear pieces in pairs. Join around edge and ladderstitch narrow edge of ear to head.

TAIL

Make one, using russet

Cast on 10sts. Beg with a k row, st-st 44 rows. **Next row:** k2 tog five times. Break off yarn, slip end through rem sts and pull tight.

With smooth sides outwards, fold tail piece in half. Join side seam, fill with stuffing and ladderstitch to back of body. Approx 2.5cm (1in) from end of tail, wrap matching yarn tightly around the tail, then fasten off securely.

SMALL WARTS

Make two, using russet

Cast on 12sts. Beg with a k row, st-st 2 rows.

Next row: k2 tog six times. **Next row:** p. Break off yarn, slip end through rem sts and pull tight.

With smooth side outwards, join shaped side seams of wart piece to form dome. Fill with stuffing and sew to nose (see picture as guide).

LARGE WARTS

Make two, using russet

Cast on 16sts. Working in st-st throughout and beg with a k row, work 2 rows.

Next row: (k2 tog, k2) four times. **Next k row:** (k2 tog, k1) four times. **Next k row:** k2 tog four times. Break off yarn, slip end through rem sts and pull tight.

Make up as for small wart and sew to nose (see picture as guide).

EYE PATCHES

Make two, using russet

Cast on 20sts. Working in st-st throughout and beg with a k row, work 2 rows.

Next row: (k2 tog, k4) three times, k2 tog. **Next k row:** (k2 tog, k2) four times. **Next k row:** (k2 tog, k1) four times. **Next k row:** k2 tog four times. Break off yarn, slip end through rem sts and pull tight.

Make up as for small wart. Fit toy safety eye in centre of patch. Fill patch with stuffing and sew to face (see picture as guide).

TUSKS

Make two, using white

Cast on 10sts. Working in st-st throughout and beg with a k row, work 2 rows.

Next row: inc one st into first st, k2, k2 tog, k2 tog, k2, inc one st into last st. **Next row:** p. Rep last 2 rows. **Next k row:** k3, k2 tog, k2 tog, k3. **Next k row:** k2, k2 tog, k2 tog, k2.

Next k row: k1, k2 tog, k2 tog, k1. **Next row:** p2 tog, p2 tog. **Next row:** k2 tog. Break off yarn, slip end through rem st and pull tight.

With smooth sides outwards, fold tusk piece in half. Join side seam, fill with stuffing and ladderstitch to side of snout, making stitches to hold tusks against snout.

NOSTRILS AND MOUTH

With black yarn, make stitches on snout for nostrils. Use straight stitches to make a mouth. Secure yarn in smooth curve with tiny stitches worked in black thread (see Basic Techniques, p11, and picture as guides).

THE SNOWY REGIONS

ESKIMO

Approximate size: 29cm (11½in)

Only human beings with great ingenuity and endurance could have survived in the cold, bleak regions of the world inhabited by Eskimos. They are native American Indians, and call themselves the 'Inuit' which means simply 'people'.

Life in the snowy regions of Canada and Alaska is very hard, and the Inuit rely on seals, whales, caribou and fish for their food and clothing, and a good sense of humour to keep them going! Where food and materials are so scarce, nothing is wasted and the people are very creative – even building cosy igloo houses out of ice and snow.

This girl is dressed in a warm sealskin coat, with furry edges to stop her face and hands getting chilly. Having just caught some fish, she is probably about to return home to her igloo for supper, accompanied by her hungry husky dog.

How easy is it to make?

Challenging. The pieces aren't too complicated, but the jacket is a bit more fiddly, with its fluffy edging and hood. If you're making this toy for a small child, you may want to sew the costume in place on the Inuit girl's body, to avoid pieces getting lost.

Tension

Over st-st, using 3¼mm (size 10, US 3) needles, 26sts and 34 rows to 10cm (4in).

Also . . .

Figures in [square brackets] give the total number of stitches or rows you should have at that stage.

The Basic Person Pattern is on p12.

All the information you need to work the Inuit Girl is in Basic Techniques, p9–13.

BODY AND HEAD
Make one, using dark brown, dark grey and skin colour
Work and make up as for Basic

Needles: 3 ¼mm (size 10, US 3)

Yarn: 50g DK in skin colour; 60g DK in dark brown; a small amount (less than 25g) in white mohair; 25g DK in black; 20g DK in chestnut brown; scraps of DK in dark grey

Pair 10mm (³/₈in) toy safety eyes

Tapestry and sewing needles

Dark brown thread

Three 10mm (³/₈in) diameter wooden beads

Washable polyester toy stuffing

Props: cardboard, glue, brown and silver paint for fish and sledge

Person Pattern, using the following colours: first 12 rows in dark brown; next 3 rows in dark grey; rem rows in skin colour.
Make up as for Basic Person Pattern.

LEGS
Make two, using chestnut brown and dark brown
Work as for Basic Person Pattern, using the following colours: first 22 rows in chestnut brown; rem rows in dark brown.
Make up as for Basic Person Pattern and ladderstitch to body.

ARMS AND EARS
Make two of each, using skin colour
Work as for Basic Person Pattern. Make up as for Basic Person Pattern and ladderstitch to body.

JACKET SLEEVES
Make two, using dark brown, with white mohair edging
Cast on 26sts in white mohair. Working in st-st throughout and beg with a k row, work 4 rows, ending with a p row.
Change to dark brown and beg with a p row, st-st 20 rows; [24 rows total]. K2 tog at both ends and once near middle of next and every foll k row until 11sts rem. **Next row:** p.
Change to white mohair and beg with a p row, work 4 rows. Cast off.
With smooth sides outwards, fold sleeve piece in half and join side seam up to start of shaping.

JACKET RIGHT FRONT
Make one, using dark brown, with white mohair edging
Cast on 14sts in white mohair. Working in st-st throughout and beg with a k row, work 4 rows, ending with a p row.
Change to dark brown and beg with a p row, work 19 rows. K2 tog at end of next and every foll k row until 8sts rem, ending with a k row. Change to white mohair and beg with a k row, work 4 rows. Cast off.

JACKET LEFT FRONT
Make one, using brown, with white mohair edging

Cast on 14sts in white mohair. Working in st-st throughout and beg with a k row, work 4 rows, ending with a p row.

Change to dark brown and beg with a p row, st-st 5 rows; [9 rows total].

The next 2 rows will make the first buttonhole, near edge of jacket front.

First buttonhole row: *k to last 3sts. From left, imagine rem sts are numbered 1, 2 & 3. K sts 3 and 2, pass st 3 over st 2 (cast it off), then k st 1.

Second buttonhole row: p2, turn and cast on one st, turn and p to end of row. Work 8 rows; [19 rows total].

To make second buttonhole, rep first and second buttonhole rows.

Work 2 rows. K2 tog at beg of next and every foll k row until 10sts rem.

To make third buttonhole, next k row: k2 tog, rep from * to end of first buttonhole row. Rep second buttonhole row.

Next row: k2 tog, k to end of row. Change to white mohair and beg with a k row, st-st 4 rows. Cast off.

Sew around buttonholes using buttonhole stitch (see Basic Techniques, p10).

JACKET BACK AND HOOD
Make one, using dark brown, with white mohair bottom edging

Cast on 32sts in white mohair. Working in st-st throughout and beg with a k row, work 4 rows, ending with a p row.

Change to brown and beg with a p row, work 19 rows.

Next row: cast off 3sts, k to end of row; [29sts]. **Next row:** cast off 3sts, p to end of row; [26sts].

K2 tog at both ends of next and every foll k row until 14sts rem. Work 3 rows.

Hood: Next row (first row of hood): cast on 6sts, k to end of row; [20sts]. **Next row:** cast on 6sts, p to end of row; [26sts]. **Next row:** k2, (inc one st into next st, k3) six times; [32sts]. **Next k row:** k3, (inc one st into next st, k4) five times, inc one st into next st, k3; [38sts]. Work 19 rows; [63 rows total].

Next k row: k2 tog, (k2 tog, k2) eight times, k2 tog, k2 tog; [27sts]. **Next k row:** (k2 tog, k1) nine times; [18sts]. **Next k row:** k2 tog nine times; [9sts]. **Next k row:** k2 tog four times, k1; [5sts]. Break off yarn, slip end through rem sts and pull tight. Hide end of yarn by sewing it back through knitting.

Lay jacket back with smooth side down. With smooth sides up, lay jacket left and right front pieces on top of jacket back, with long straight edges of front pieces overlapping in the centre.

Join side seams up to start of shaping. Position sleeves on either side of jacket and join sleeves to armholes of jacket.

Join mohair edging where it meets.

HOOD EDGING
Make one, using white mohair

Cast on 54sts. Work 4 rows in st-st. Cast off.

Sew edging piece to front edge of hood (see picture on p111 as guide).

HAIR
Work top of hair as for Basic Person Pattern, using black and making matching plaits, with hair ties in chestnut yarn.

MOUTH
Work as for Basic Person Pattern, using dark brown yarn.

FINISHING TOUCHES
Sledge Cut out four rectangles of cardboard, 15cm (6in) by 10cm (4in). Stick rectangles together to form piece thick enough for sledge top. Paint this piece brown. Trace sledge runner pattern (below) on to paper, cut it out and draw round it twice on thick cardboard. Cut out cardboard runners and paint them silver. Fold top section of runner (along dotted line) and stick top section to underside of sledge top. Rep for second runner. If runners are wobbly, stick more card to underside of sledge between runners.

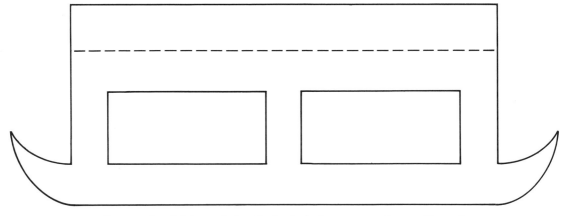

Runner for Eskimo sledge (actual size) – cut two in cardboard

HUSKY DOG

Approximate size: 20.5cm (8 1/4in)

People have always had a special friendship with dogs. From at least as far back as historical records have been kept, dogs have been a part of people's lives. They have not always been simply pets, but also hunting, farm and guard dogs.

The Eskimo or Inuit people also found a good friend in dogs. The huskies, with their thick coats and incredible stamina, are ideal companions in countries where the temperature is often well below freezing point. Teams of huskies can be used to pull sledges, helping people to move swiftly across vast open expanses of snow.

This little husky dog isn't much more than a puppy, so may not be able to pull very much on his own. But with his bright eyes and smiling face, his enthusiasm will make up for what he lacks in strength!

How easy is it to make?

Easy! It's quick to knit, with a few simple pieces. If you don't like working with fluffy mohair, try knitting this husky in DK yarn instead.

Needles: 3 3/4mm (size 9, US 4)

Yarn: 25g DK in light grey mohair; 25g DK in white mohair; scraps of DK in black

Pair of 10mm (3/8in) toy safety eyes

Tapestry needle

Washable polyester toy stuffing

Props: 3 1/4mm (size 10, US 3) needles and scraps of brightly-coloured and black DK for the fish; scraps of brown yarn for the sledge harness

Tension

Over st-st, using 3 3/4mm (size 9, US 4) needles, 18sts and 28 rows to 10cm (4in).

Also . . .

Figures in [square brackets] give the total number of stitches or rows you should have at that stage.

All the information you need to work the Husky Dog is in Basic Techniques, p9–13.

BASE OF BODY AND HEAD
Make one, using white

Cast on 12sts. This is the tail end. Working in st-st throughout, and beg with a k row, work 2 rows.

Next row: k5, inc one st into next 2sts, k5. **Next k row:** k6, inc one st into next 2sts, k6; [16sts]. Work 19 rows; [24 rows total].

Next row: k6, k2 tog, k2 tog, k6. **Next k row:** k5, k2 tog, k2 tog, k5. **Next k row:** k4, k2 tog, k2 tog, k4; [10sts]. Work 3 rows; [32 rows total].

Next row: k4, inc one st into next 2sts, k4. **Next k row:** k5, inc one st into next 2sts, k5; [14sts]. Work 3 rows; [38 rows total].

Next row: k5, k2 tog, k2 tog, k5. **Next k row:** k4, k2 tog, k2 tog, k4, [10sts].* Mark both ends of this row with coloured yarn.

Next k row: cast on 3sts, k to end of row. **Next row:** cast on 3sts, p to end of row; [16sts]. Work 2 rows. **Next row:** (k2, k2 tog) twice, (k2 tog, k2) twice; [12sts]. **Next k row:** (k1, k2 tog) twice, (k2 tog, k1) twice; [8sts]. **Next k row:** k2 tog four times; [4sts]. Cast off.

TOP OF BODY AND HEAD
Make one, using light grey

Work as for base of body and head to *. **Next k row:** k3, k2 tog, k2 tog, k3; [8sts]. **Next row:** p. Cast off. This is the head end. With smooth sides outwards, join base and top pieces along straight seam.

Match end of grey piece with coloured marker on white piece (see diagram). Rep for other side of husky.

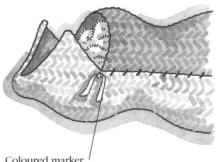

Coloured marker

Join tops of two flaps forming husky's snout. Fold top edge of snout up to head and sew in place. Fill snout, head and body with stuffing, then sew closed. Remove coloured markers.

TAIL

Make one, using light grey

Cast on 10sts. Working in st-st throughout and beg with a k row, work 4 rows. **Next row:** inc one st into first st, k8, inc one st into last st; [12sts]. Work 9 rows; [14 rows total]. K2 tog at both ends of next and every foll k row until 2sts rem. Cast off.

With smooth sides outwards, fold tail piece in half. Join long curved seam, fill with a little stuffing, then ladderstitch to body.

LEGS

Make four, using white

Cast on 8sts. P 1 row. **Next row:** inc one st into first st, k2, inc one st into next 2sts, k2, inc one st into last st. Work 15 rows; [17 rows total]. Cast off.

With smooth sides outwards, fold leg piece in half. Starting at cast on end, join end of foot and straight seam. Fill with stuffing and sew closed. Ladderstitch to body.

Paws: on each leg, bend up a paw at right angles to leg and ladderstitch in position (see diagram below).

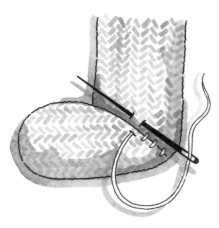

EARS

Make two, using white; and two, using grey

Cast on 5sts. Beg with a p row, st-st 5 rows. **Next row:** k2 tog, k1, k2 tog; [3sts]. **Next row:** p. **Next row:** k3 tog. Break off yarn, slip end through rem st and pull tight.

With smooth sides outwards, match up white ear piece with grey ear piece. Join around edge, then ladderstitch ear to head with white side facing forwards.

EYE PATCHES

Make two, using white

Cast on 5sts. Beg with a k row, st-st 4 rows. **Next row:** k2 tog, k1, k2 tog; [3sts]. **Next row:** p. Cast off.

Position and fit toy safety eyes through eye patches (see Basic Techniques, p8). Sew eye patches on grey part of husky's face, just above snout (see picture on p110 as guide), pushing shanks of eyes into head. Fill snout, head and body with stuffing through open tail end and sew closed. Remove coloured markers.

NOSE, MOUTH AND CLAWS

With black yarn, make three stitches on end of snout for a nose. Sew an upside-down T shape under nose for mouth. On each paw, sew three big stitches for claws (see Basic Techniques, p11, and picture on p110 as guides).

VARIATIONS

The husky looks very much like an Alsatian dog, which isn't surprising since they're both closely related to the wolf. To make an Alsatian puppy, follow the husky pattern, using the following colours: work legs, base of body and head, and fronts of ears using mid brown; work top of body and head, tail and backs of ears in black.

FISH

BODY, HEAD AND TAIL

Cast on 14sts. Beg with a k row, st-st 16 rows. **Next row:** k2 tog seven times. Break off yarn, slip end through rem sts and pull tight.

With smooth sides outwards, fold body, head and tail piece in half and join along side seam. Fill with stuffing then sew closed.

Approx 1cm (1/2 in) from straight end, wind matching yarn around body and pull tight to form tail. At right angles to this line of yarn, gather in the tail section in the middle with a few stitches and fasten off securely.

For eyes, embroider two spots in black yarn.

PENGUINS

Approximate sizes: Adult Emperor 24cm (9 1/2 in); Emperor Chick 15.5cm (6 1/2 in); Adult Adélie 23cm (9in); Adélie Chick 14cm (5 1/2 in)

Penguins have a strong family loyalty which is put to the test throughout the bitter Antarctic winter. Before the coldest weather, the female penguins lay one large egg and then disappear into the sea to feed. The males are left on their own to look after the egg, which they dutifully carry balanced on their feet to keep it warm. Only when the female returns will the male finally go off to find some food for himself.

With just simple variations of colours and markings, you can make different species of penguin using one pattern for an adult and one for a baby penguin. Very soon, you could have a whole flock of these comical little birds!

How easy is it to make?

Straightforward. The pieces are easy to knit, with only minimal colour changes to represent the markings. The making up and finishing stages for each penguin may require a little more concentration.

For all penguins

Needles: 3 1/4 mm (size 10, US 3)

Pair 10mm (3/8 in) toy safety eyes

Tapestry needle

Washable polyester toy stuffing

For an adult Emperor penguin

Yarn: 40g DK in black, 25g DK in white; scraps of DK in dark brown, orange and yellow

For an adult Adélie penguin

Yarn: 40g DK in black; 25g DK in white; scraps of DK in dark grey

For an Emperor penguin chick

Yarn: 10g DK in grey mohair; scraps of DK in black, dark brown and white

For an Adélie penguin chick

Yarn: 10g DK in light brown mohair; scraps of DK in dark brown

Tension

Over st-st, using 3 1/4 mm (size 10, US 3) needles, 26sts and 34 rows to 10cm (4in).

Also . . .

Figures in [square brackets] give the total number of stitches or rows you should have at that stage.

All the information you need to work the Penguins is in Basic Techniques, p9–13.

ADULT PENGUIN

BACK AND HEAD
Make one, using black
Cast on 48sts. Working in st-st throughout and beg with a k row, work 2 rows. **Next row:** k(22), k2 tog, k2 tog, k to end of row. **Next row:** p. Rep last 2 rows, with number of sts in brackets 1 less each time, until 30sts rem. Work 27 rows; [46 rows total].
Next row: inc one st into first st, k12, k2 tog, k2 tog, k to last st, inc one st into last st. **Next row:** p; [30sts]. Rep last 2 rows seven more times; [62 rows total]. Mark both ends of last row with coloured yarn.

Inc one st at both ends of next and every foll k row until you have 36sts total. Work 5 rows; [72 rows total].
Next row: k2 tog, k(14), k2 tog, k2 tog, k to last 2sts, k2 tog. **Next row:** p. Rep last 2 rows, with number of sts in brackets 2 less each time, until 20sts rem.
Next row: (p2 tog, p6, p2 tog) twice; [16sts]. Cast off.

STOMACH
Make one, using white (with yellow and orange for Emperor penguin)
Cast on 2sts. Working in st-st throughout and beg with a k row, work 2 rows. **Next row:** inc one st into both sts. Inc one st at both ends of next and every foll k row until you have 20sts total. Work 43 rows; [62 rows total].
For an Adélie penguin, cont work in white; for an Emperor penguin, change to yellow.
K2 tog at both ends of next and every foll k row until 14sts rem.
For an Adélie penguin, cont work in white; for an Emperor penguin, change to orange.

K2 tog at both ends of next and every foll k row until 10sts rem. **Next k row:** k2 tog, k2 tog, k2, k2 tog, k2 tog. **Next k row:** k2 tog three times. **Next row:** p. Cast off.

With smooth sides outwards, fold black body piece in half lengthways. The point that sticks out at the back is the tail. Take fat pointed end of stomach piece (white end for Emperor penguin) and join it, using black yarn, to point of tail. Join one side of stomach piece to back piece, matching second point of stomach to coloured marker at neck. Rep for other side of stomach.

Join front of head. Position and fit safety eyes on each side of face. Fill with stuffing and sew closed. Remove coloured markers.

WINGS

Make one piece A using black; one piece A using white; one piece B using black; one piece B using white

Piece A – Cast on 12sts. Working in st-st throughout and beg with a k row, work 10 rows. **Next row:** inc one st into first st, k to last 2sts, k2 tog. **Next row:** p. Rep last 2 rows three more times; [18 rows total].

Next row: k2 tog, k to last st, inc one st into last st. **Next row:** p. Rep last 2 rows twice more; [24 rows total].

K2 tog at beg of next and every foll k row until 6sts rem. **Next k row:** k2 tog, k2, k2 tog. Cast off.

Piece B – Cast on 12sts. Working in st-st throughout and beg with a k row, work 10 rows. **Next row:** k2 tog, k to last st, inc one st into last st. **Next row:** p. Rep last 2 rows three more times; [18 rows total].

Next row: inc one st into first st, k to last 2sts, k2 tog. **Next row:** p. Rep last 2 rows twice more; [24 rows total].

K2 tog at end of next and every foll k row until 6sts rem. **Next k row:** k2 tog, k2, k2 tog. Cast off.

With smooth sides outwards, match up wing pieces in pairs – one white and one black in each pair, and join two pieces together around edge. Ladderstitch straight edge of wing to side of body (see picture as guide).

EMPEROR PENGUIN BEAK
Make one, using dark brown

Cast on 9sts. Working in st-st throughout and beg with a k row, work 10 rows. **Next row:** inc one st into first st, (k1, k2 tog) twice, k1, inc one st into last st. **Next k row:** k2, k2 tog, k1, k2 tog, k2. **Next k row:** (k1, k2 tog) twice, k1. **Next k row:** k2 tog, k1, k2 tog. **Next k row:** k3 tog. Break off yarn, slip end through rem st and pull tight.

With smooth sides outwards, fold beak piece in half. Join side seam, fill with stuffing then ladderstitch to front of face.

ADÉLIE PENGUIN BEAK
Make one, using grey

Cast on 10sts. Working in st-st throughout and beg with a k row, work 8 rows. **Next row:** (k2 tog, k1, k2 tog) twice. **Next k row:** k2 tog three times. **Next k row:** k3 tog. Break off yarn, slip end through rem st and pull tight.

Make up as for Emperor penguin beak and ladderstitch to front of face.

TOES
Make six, using dark brown for Emperor penguin; using grey for Adélie penguin

Cast on 8sts. Beg with a k row, st-st 12 rows. **Next row:** k2 tog, k to last 2sts, k2 tog. **Next row:** p. Rep last 2 rows. Cast off.

With smooth sides outwards, fold toe piece in half. Join side seam, fill with stuffing and sew closed.

Foot: Sew 3 toes together with ladderstitch, working a little way up towards points of toes each time to make them point forwards. Ladderstitch to base of penguin.

Finishing the penguins

HEAD MARKINGS FOR EMPEROR PENGUIN
Make two, using orange

Cast on 4sts. P 1 row. Working in st-st throughout, next row: inc one st into first st, k2, inc one st into last st. Work 9 rows; [11 rows total]. **Next row:** k2 tog, k to last 2sts, k2 tog. Work 3 rows. Rep last 4 rows; [2sts]. **Next row:** k2 tog. Break off yarn, slip end through rem st and pull tight. This end will meet the other head marking at the top point of the stomach.

With smooth side outwards, sew head marking pieces to sides of head, with points meeting at top of stomach piece (see picture as guide).

With orange yarn, make markings on sides of beak with lines of chainstitch (see Basic Techniques, p10).

EYE MARKINGS FOR ADÉLIE PENGUIN

With white yarn, chainstitch pointed eye shape around each eye (see Basic Techniques, p10, and picture as guides).

BODY AND HEAD FOR PENGUIN CHICKS

Make one, using grey and black for Emperor penguin chick; using light brown for Adélie penguin chick

Cast on 24sts (in grey for Emperor penguin chick; light brown for Adélie penguin chick). P 1 row. Working in st-st throughout, next row: k8, inc one st into next st, k6, inc one st into next st, k8; [26sts]. **Next k row:** inc one st into first st, k7, inc one st into next 2sts, k6, inc one st into next 2sts, k7, inc one st into last; [32sts]. **Next k row:** inc one st into first st, k9, inc one st into next 2sts, k8, inc one st into next 2sts, k9, inc one st into last st; [38sts]. Work 3 rows.

K2 tog at both ends of next and every foll k row until 18sts rem, ending with a p row.

For Emperor penguin chick, cont as foll: change to black and beg with a p row, work 9 rows. **Next row:** (k2 tog, k5, k2 tog) twice; [14sts]. **Next row:** p. Cast off.

For Adélie penguin chick, cont in light brown as foll: beg with a k row, work 8 rows; [37 rows total].

Next row: (k2 tog, k5, k2 tog) twice; [14sts]. **Next row:** p. Cast off.

With smooth sides of body together, fold body and head piece in half. Using matching yarn, join top of head and side seam. For Adélie penguin chick, position and fit toy safety eyes. Fill body and head with stuffing.

BASE

Make one, using grey for Emperor penguin chick; using light brown for Adélie penguin chick

Cast on 6sts. Working in st-st throughout, and beg with a k row, work 2 rows. **Next row:** inc one st into first st, k to last st, inc one st into last st. **Next row:** p. Rep last 2 rows; [10sts]. Work 8 rows; [14 rows total].

Next row: k2 tog, k to last 2sts, k2 tog. **Next row:** p. Rep last 2 rows; [6sts]. Cast off.

With smooth side inwards, cover hole at bottom of penguin chick with base piece. Sew in place.

EMPEROR PENGUIN CHICK WINGS

Make two, using grey

Cast on 14sts. Working in st-st throughout and beg with a k row, work 8 rows. **Next row:** inc one st into first st, k4, k2 tog, k2 tog, k4, inc one st into last st. **Next row:** p. Rep last 2 rows three more times; [16 rows total].

K2 tog at both ends of next and every foll k row until 8sts rem. **Next k row:** (k2 tog, k1) twice, k2 tog. **Next row:** p. Cast off.

With smooth sides together, fold wing piece in half and join around edge. Ladderstitch to side of chick's body.

ADÉLIE PENGUIN CHICK WINGS

Make two, using light brown

Cast on 14sts. Working in st-st throughout and beg with a k row, work 12 rows.

K2 tog at both ends of next and every foll k row until 8sts rem. **Next row:** p. Cast off.

Make up as for Emperor penguin chick's wing and ladderstitch to body.

BEAK FOR BOTH CHICKS

Make one, using dark brown

Cast on 7sts. Working in st-st throughout and beg with a k row, work 4 rows. K2 tog at both ends of next and every foll k row until 3sts rem. **Next k row:** k3 tog. Break off yarn, slip end through rem st and pull tight.

With smooth sides outwards, fold beak piece in half. Join along side seam, fill with stuffing then ladderstitch to front of chick's face.

Finishing the penguin chick

EMPEROR PENGUIN CHICK EYE PATCHES

Make two, using white

Cast on 3sts. P 1 row. Working in st-st throughout, next row: inc one st into first st, k1, inc one st into last st. **Next k row:** inc one st into first st, k3, inc one st into last st; [7sts]. Work 3 rows.

Next row: k2 tog, k3, k2 tog. **Next k row:** k2 tog, k1, k2 tog; [3sts]. **Next row:** p. Cast off.

Position and fit a toy safety eye in the centre of each eye patch. With white yarn, ladderstitch eye patches to sides of chick's head (see picture on p116 as guide).

FEET FOR BOTH CHICKS

Make a 15cm (6in) single chain in DK yarn (see Basic Techniques, p10). Sew chain to base of penguin in three toe loops. Sew loops closed with extra stitches in yarn (see diagram below). Rep for second foot.

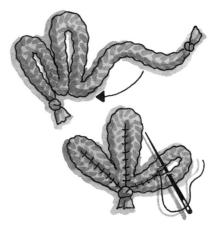

SEAL

Approximate size: 24cm (9 1/2 in)

Seals are intelligent and inquisitive creatures that will often show a great deal of interest in human activity. They look just like bathers enjoying the sun, bobbing about in the water, or gazing around at the fishermen or holidaymakers who share their seaside world. With their wide-set eyes and huge smiling mouths, they can look uncannily like people, so it's not surprising that in many cultures there are folk stories about seals having human spirits trapped inside them. There are even stories of Selkies – women in seal form – who can only be persuaded to stay on dry land if their magical sealskin is hidden away from them.

Knitted in soft mohair, these friendly little seals have just the same great big eyes, irresistible smiles and inquisitive natures. They are the simplest of all the toys to make with just four separate pieces – all knitted in the same yarn.

How easy is it to make?

Easy! This is a great toy for beginners to make – four simple pieces in a single colour. If you don't like working in fluffy mohair, smooth DK yarn works well, too.

Needles: 3mm (size 11, US 2)

Yarn: 50g DK in white mohair; scraps of DK in black

Pair 16mm (5/8 mm) black toy safety eyes

Tapestry and sewing needles

Black thread

Washable polyester toy stuffing

Tension

Over st-st, using 3mm (size 11, US 2) needles, 28sts and 36 rows to 10cm (4in).

Also . . .

Figures in [square brackets] give the total number of stitches or rows you should have at that stage.

All the information you need to work the Seal is in Basic Techniques, p9–13.

BODY AND HEAD
Make one, using white
Cast on 16sts. Working in st-st throughout, and beg with a k row, work 2 rows.
Next row: inc one st into first st, k(6), inc one st into next 2sts, k to last st, inc one st into last st. Work 3 rows. Rep last 4 rows, with number of sts in brackets 2 more each time, until you have 44sts total. Work 43 rows; [70 rows total].
*****Next row:** k2 tog, (k18), k2 tog, k2 tog, k to last 2sts, k2 tog. **Next row:** p. Rep last 2 rows, with number of sts in brackets 2 less each time, until 24sts rem. Work 5 rows; [84 rows total].
Next row: (k2 tog, k2 tog, k4, k2 tog, k2 tog) twice; [16sts]. **Next k row:** (k2 tog, k4, k2 tog) twice; [12sts]. Break off yarn, slip end through rem sts and pull tight. This is the nose end.
With smooth sides together, fold body and head piece in half. Join long side seam. Position and fit toy safety eyes, fill with stuffing, then sew closed.
Snout: about 2.5cm (1in) from nose end, sew a line of running stitch in matching yarn around nose, and pull tight (see Basic Techniques, p11). Secure end of yarn by making a few stitches.
Head: about 7.5cm (3in) from nose end, make a neck using the same technique as for the snout.

TAIL FLIPPER
Make one, using white
Cast on 18sts. This is the end to attach later to the body. Working in st-st throughout and beg with a k row, work 2 rows.
Next row: inc one st into first st, k(7), inc one st into next 2sts, k to last st, inc one st into last st. **Next row:** p. Rep last 2 rows, with number of sts in brackets 2 more each time, until you have 42sts total. **Next row:** p. Cast off.
With smooth sides together, fold tail flipper piece in half. Join around two edges, fill with a little stuffing, then sew closed. Ladderstitch flipper to tail end of seal (see picture on p109 as guide).

FRONT FLIPPERS
Make two, using white
Cast on 16sts. Working in st-st throughout, and beg with a k row, work 4 rows.
Next row: inc one st into first 2sts, k to last 2sts, inc one st

into last 2sts. **Next row:** p. Rep last 2 rows until you have 28sts total. Work 3 rows. Cast off.
With smooth sides together, fold front flipper piece in half. Join around two edges, fill with a little stuffing, then ladderstitch to side of seal (see picture on p109 as guide). Make extra stitches to hold flipper against body.

NOSE AND MOUTH

With black yarn, make three stitches on end of snout for a nose. Sew a big upside-down T shape under nose for a mouth. Secure yarn in a smooth curve with tiny stitches worked in black thread (see Basic Techniques, p11, and picture on p109 as guides).

WALRUS

Approximate size: 40cm (16in)

Walruses are extremely friendly creatures and are often seen flopping about together in huge gatherings on the land. They are immensely fat, equipped with a thick layer of blubber to keep out the cold. But their huge weight can make life very difficult when trying to get out of the water, so they use their tusks to lever themselves on to the rocks.

As well as being social, walruses are also very competitive. They fight over mates and can cause serious injury with their tusks. A walrus's status in the society is clearly on display – the bigger your tusks, the more important you are. So this knitted walrus probably ranks somewhere in the middle!

How easy is it to make?

Straightforward. The pieces are simple to make – only the tusks might prove a little more challenging. They have a tendency to point in the wrong directions! So pay particular attention when attaching the tusks.

Needles: 3 ³/₄mm (size 9, US 4); for tusks 3mm (size 11, US 2)

Yarn: 60g DK in mid brown; a small amount (approx 10g) DK in white; scraps of DK in black

Pair 14mm (¹/₂ in) toy safety eyes

Tapestry and sewing needles

Black thread

Washable polyester toy stuffing

Tension

Over st-st, using 3 ³/₄m (size 9, US 4) needles, 18sts and 28 rows to 10cm (4in).

Over st-st, using 3mm (size 11, US 2) needles, 28sts and 36 rows to 10cm (4in).

Also . . .

Figures in [square brackets] give the total number of stitches or rows you should have at that stage.

All the information you need to work the Walrus is in Basic Techniques, p9–13.

BODY AND HEAD

Make one, using mid brown

Cast on 16sts. Working in st-st throughout, and beg with a k row, work 2 rows.

Next row: inc one st into first st, k(6), inc one st into next 2sts, k to last st, inc one st into last st. Work 3 rows. Rep last 4 rows, with number of sts in brackets 2 more each time, until you have 44sts total. Work 81 rows; [108 rows total].

Work as for seal body and head (see p119), from * to end.

Head: Approx 7.5cm (3in) from nose end, bend head downwards at shallow angle to neck. Join chin to front of neck with ladderstitch.

Chest: Approx 15cm (6in) from nose end, bend neck upwards at shallow angle to body. Join back of neck to top of body with ladderstitch.

Snout: Approx 2.5cm (1in) from nose end, sew a line of running stitch (see Basic Techniques, p11) in matching yarn around the nose, and pull gently. Secure end of yarn by making a few stitches.

TAIL FLIPPER

Make one, using mid brown

Cast on 18sts. This is the end to attach to the body. Working in st-st throughout, and beg with a k row, work 4 rows.

Next row: inc one st into first st, k(7), inc one st into next 2sts, k to last st, inc one st into last st. **Next row:** p. Rep last 2 rows, with number of sts in brackets 2 more each time, until you have 42sts total. Work 3 rows. Cast off.

With smooth sides together, fold tail flipper piece in half. Join around two edges, fill with a little stuffing, then sew closed. Ladderstitch flipper to tail end of walrus (see picture as guide). Sew a line of running stitch halfway down middle of tail, from long straight edge.

FRONT FLIPPERS

Make two, using mid brown

Cast on 16sts. Working in st-st throughout and beg with a k row, work 4 rows. Inc one st at both ends of next and every foll k row until you have 30sts total. Work 3 rows. Cast off.

With smooth sides outwards, fold front flipper piece in half. Join around curved edge, fill lightly with stuffing, then sew hole closed. Ladderstitch flipper to side of chest (see picture as guide). Make extra stitches to hold flipper against body. On each flipper, sew three lines of stitching (see diagram below).

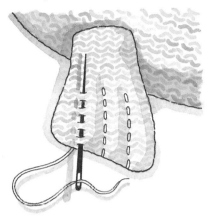

NOSE AND MOUTH

With black yarn, make three stitches on end of snout for a nose. Sew one stitch down from nose, and two big lines from bottom of this stitch as a mouth. Secure yarn in a smooth curve with tiny stitches worked in black thread (see Basic Techniques, p11).

TUSKS

Make two, using 3mm (size 11, US 2) needles and white

Cast on 10sts. Working in st-st throughout and beg with a k row, work 12 rows.

Next row: inc one st into first st, k2, k2 tog, k2 tog, k2, inc one st into last st. **Next row:** p. Rep last 2 rows three more times; [20 rows total].

Next row: k3, k2 tog, k2 tog, k3. **Next k row:** k2, k2 tog, k2 tog, k2. **Next k row:** k1, k2 tog, k2 tog, k1. **Next row:** p. Cast off.

With smooth sides outwards, fold tusk piece in half. Join along curved edge, fill with stuffing then sew closed. Ladderstitch under black line of mouth. Make extra stitches to hold tusks against chin.

POLAR BEAR

Approximate size: 29cm (11¹/₂ in)

Despite their size, polar bears are agile and graceful, and are able to move equally well in the water as they do on the land or ice. They mainly hunt seals, which are fast movers and alert to danger. So the polar bears are equipped with dense white fur, which not only camouflages them in the snowy landscape, but also keeps them from freezing when they dive after their prey into the icy water.

Over the bitter winters, mother polar bears hollow out caves in the snow. These are where the cubs are born and protected through the first months of their lives. So it is not until spring comes that the baby polar bears get their first glimpse of the white world which will be their home.

With her round, chubby shape, this cuddly polar bear looks as if she'd like to stay in a cosy cave rather than venture out into an Arctic spring!

How easy is it to make?

Straightforward. There's some shaping on the nose and head, but nothing too complicated.

Needles: 3 ¹/₄ mm (size 10, US 3)

Yarn: 100g DK in white; scraps of DK in dark brown

Pair 4mm (¹/₂ in) toy safety eyes

Tapestry and sewing needles

Black thread

Washable polyester toy stuffing

Tension

Over st-st, using 3 ¹/₄ mm (size 10, US 3) needles, 26sts and 34 rows to 10cm (4in).

Also . . .

Figures in [square brackets] give the total number of stitches or rows you should have at that stage.

All the information you need to work the Polar Bear is in Basic Techniques, p9–13.

BODY AND HEAD
Make one, using white

Cast on 24sts. P1 row. Working in st-st throughout, next row: inc one st into first 2sts, k(8), inc one st into next 4sts, k to last 2sts, inc one st into last 2sts. **Next row:** p. Rep last 2 rows, with number of sts in brackets 4 more each time, until you have 72sts total.

Next k row: inc one st into first st, k34, inc one st into next 2sts, k to last st, inc one st into last st; [76sts].Work 15 rows; [29 rows total].

Next row: k2 tog, k(34), k2 tog, k2 tog, k to last 2sts, k2 tog. **Next row:** p. Rep last 2 rows, with number of sts in brackets 2 less each time, until 60sts rem. Work 7 rows; [43 rows total].

Next row: k29, inc one st into next 2sts, k29.

Next k row: k(29), inc one st into next 4sts, k to end of row. **Next row:** p. Rep last 2 rows, with number of sts in brackets 2 more each time, until you have 78sts total. Work 3 rows; [55 rows total].

K2 tog at both ends of next and every foll k row until 72sts rem.

Next k row: k2 tog, k(32), k2 tog, k2 tog, k to last 2sts, k2 tog. **Next row:** p. Rep last 2 rows, with number of sts in brackets 2 less each time, until 48sts rem.

Next k row: k(22), k2 tog, k2 tog, k to end of row. **Next row:** p. Rep last 2 rows, with number of sts in brackets 1 less each time, until 40sts rem.

Next k row: (k2 tog, k2 tog, k12, k2 tog, k2 tog) twice; [32sts]. Work 7 rows; [89 rows total].

Next row: k2 tog, k2 tog, k to last 4sts, k2 tog, k2 tog. **Next row:** p. Rep last 2 rows until 20sts rem. **Next row:** p. Cast off. This is the nose end.

With smooth sides outwards, fold body and head piece in half. Join nose end and long seam. Position and fit toy safety eyes, fill body and head with stuffing, then sew closed.

LEGS
Make four, using white

Cast on 14sts. This is the paw end.

Working in st-st throughout and beg with a k row, work 2 rows.

Next row: inc one st into first st, k(5), inc one st into next 2sts, k to last st, inc one st into last st. **Next row:** p. Rep last 2 rows, with number of sts in brackets 2 more each time, until you have 30sts total. Work 41 rows; [50 rows total]. Cast off.

With smooth sides outwards, fold leg piece in half. Join end of foot and long side seam, fill with stuffing then sew closed. Ladderstitch leg to body.

Paws: 5cm (2in) up from end of leg, bend paw up at right angles to leg and ladderstitch in position.

EARS
Make two, using white
Cast on 28sts. Working in st-st throughout, and beg with a k row, work 10 rows.
Next row: (k2 tog, k10, k2 tog) twice; [24sts]. **Next k row:** (k2 tog, k8, k2 tog) twice; [20sts]. **Next k row:** (k2 tog, k6, k2 tog) twice; [16sts]. **Next row:** p. Cast off.
With smooth sides outwards, fold ear piece in half. Join around edge then ladderstitch to head.

TAIL
Make one, using white
Cast on 10sts. Working in st-st throughout and beg with a k row, work 6 rows. **Next row:** (k2 tog, k1, k2 tog) twice; [6sts]. **Next k row:** k2 tog three times; [3sts]. **Next k row:** k3 tog. Break off yarn, slip end through rem sts and pull tight. Hide end of yarn by sewing it back through knitting.
With smooth side outwards, sew tail to back of bear.

NOSE AND MOUTH
With dark brown yarn, make a few stitches on end of snout as nose. Sew one stitch down from nose, and two lines out from bottom of this stitch as a mouth. Secure yarn in a smooth curve with tiny stitches worked in black thread (see Basic Techniques, p11).

PATTERN VARIATIONS

With simple colour variations, some of the patterns in this book can be turned into other animals. Here, the polar bear pattern has been used to create a panda, and the walrus has been used to create a sea lion.

SEA LION

Approximate size: 40cm (16in)

Famous for their circus performances, sea lions are agile and intelligent. They are able to follow even quite complicated instructions from the circus ringmaster. But these skills weren't developed merely to entertain human beings. In the wild, sea lions need their agility and skill in underwater acrobatics to catch up with the fast-moving fish that are their food.

How easy is it to make?

Easy! There are only four pieces to knit, all of them very simple. Only the shaping of the head (involving some neat sewing) might take some practice.

Tension

Over st-st, using 3 3/4mm (size 9, US 4) needles, 18sts and 28 rows to 10cm (4in).

Also . . .

Work as for the walrus (p120), working all pieces in black, and leaving out tusks.

All the information you need to work the Sea Lion is in Basic Techniques, p9–13.

Needles: 3 3/4 mm (size 9, US 4)

Yarn: 60g DK in black yarn: scraps of DK yarn in dark grey for nose and mouth

A pair of 14mm (1/2 in) toy safety eyes

Tapestry and sewing needles

Black thread

Washable polyester toy stuffing

Instructions for the fish in this picture can be found on p114.

PANDA

Approximate size: 29cm (11½in)

Pandas are often called bears, even though their closest living relative is actually the raccoon. In China, where pandas are found in the wild, they are known as the snow bear, and there is a traditional story of how they got their black and white markings. It is said that the pandas were once pure white, and were looked after by a beautiful Chinese girl. When she died, the pandas cried so much that the dye from their black armbands stained their arms and legs. When they covered their ears to shut out the story of the girl's death, their ears became black. And when they rubbed their tear-filled eyes, they gained their familiar black eye patches.

How easy is it to make?

Straightforward. There's some shaping on the nose and head, but nothing too complicated.

Needles: 3 ¼mm (size 10, US 3)

Yarn: 50g DK in white; 50g DK in black; scraps of DK yarn in dark brown

A pair of 4mm (½ in) toy safety eyes

Tapestry and sewing needles

Black thread

Washable polyester toy stuffing

Tension

Over **st-st**, using 3 ¼mm (size 10, US 3) needles, 26sts and 34 rows to 10cm (4in).

Also . . .

Work as for the polar bear (p122), using the following colours: body and head piece in white; legs, ears, and tail in black. Then follow instructions above right for eye patches.

All the information you need to work the Panda is in Basic Techniques, p9–13.

EYE PATCHES
Make two, using black
Cast on 4sts. Working in st-st throughout and beg with a k row, work 2 rows. Inc one st at both ends of next and every foll k row until you have 10sts total. Work 11 rows. K2 tog at both ends of next and every foll k row until 4sts rem. **Next row**: p. Cast off.

Follow instructions for finishing polar bear, but do not fit eyes. Instead, position and fit toy safety eye in eye patch, close to end (see picture below as guide). Sew eye patch to panda's face, pushing shank of eye into panda's head. Rep for second eye patch.

Suppliers

It's good to use up scraps of wool left over from bigger projects, so take a look in your own wool collection before spending money on new yarn for your toys. Also, ask family and friends to donate their own odds and ends – each oddment of yarn will be sure to come with its own history, which can add to your enjoyment of making the toy.

If you want to buy new yarn, then I recommend searching out the small specialist yarn shops which exist in almost every town. They are usually run by friendly enthusiasts, who will often take the trouble to help you choose a suitable yarn, or dig out unusual oddments from the stock cupboard. Many of these shops will also have a basket of odds and ends of yarn, suitable for toy-making, at reduced prices. Much of the yarn used for toys in this book came from just such baskets in wool shops in Totnes, Exeter and Great Torrington in Devon.

If you live in a city, then you'll find that many big department stores, such as John Lewis and Debenhams, have good yarn departments, with an extensive choice of colours and makes.

If you can't get to any of these shops, then you may like to contact the manufacturers directly. The main manufacturers are listed below. Please note that no one make or supplier of yarn was used for the toys in this book. My own preference is to choose yarns for their colour and texture. With toys, it is not essential to match makes or even types of yarn, and unusual combinations of textures (such as for the sheep and wombat in this book) can often give interesting effects.

Jaeger Handknits
Green Mill Lane
Holmfirth
West Yorkshire
HD7 1RW

Patons (Diploma)
Patons and Baldwin Ltd.
Darlington PO Box 22
The Lingfield Estate
McMullen Road
Darlington
Co. Durham
DL1 1YQ

Jonelle Knitting Yarns
John Lewis Partnership
171 Victoria Street
London
SW1E 5NW

Sirdar plc
Flanshaw Lane
Wakefield
West Yorkshire
WF2 9ND

Wendy/Peter Pan
Carter and Parker Ltd
Guiseley
Yorkshire

Rowan Yarns
Green Lane Mill
Holmfirth
West Yorkshire
HD7 1RW

Hayfield Textiles Ltd
Flanshaw Lane
Alverthorpe
Wakefield
West Yorkshire
WF2 9ND

ACKNOWLEDGEMENTS

I would like to thank the following people for their contributions to the creation of this book.

My good friend Hilary Nicholson, for her tireless knitting and unfailing good humour, even in the midst of requests for dozens of woolly arms and legs. Without her help and support this book would not have been possible.

Frances Kelly, Jenny Rodwell, Cheryl Brown and Mary Bartlett, for their expert advice and support.

Brenda Morrison and Alan Duns, for excellent creative weekends of photography, unfailing hospitality, good food and the opportunity to see beautiful trees.

The Mesdames Desfarges (Inge, Hilary, Jo and Wendy), for knitting evenings and good company.

Sally Carr Designs in Totnes, my favourite wool shop, who never knew they were taking part in this venture, but who always helped out with interesting yarns and a friendly welcome.

All the staff at Schumacher College, for their continued support of my crazy projects, and for kindly recognising the knitted animals as they emerged.

Marcelle Shears, who first inspired me to take make something of my love of craft, and to whom I will always be grateful.

INDEX

Page numbers in *italic* indicate photographs